If These WALLS *Could* TALK:

SAN FRANCISCO GIANTS

Stories from the
San Francisco Giants Dugout,
Locker Room, and Press Box

Chris Haft

TRIUMPH
BOOKS

Library of Congress Cataloging-in-Publication Data available upon request

This book is available in quantity at special discounts for your group or organization. For further information, contact:

Triumph Books LLC
814 North Franklin Street
Chicago, Illinois 60610
www.triumphbooks.com

Printed in U.S.A.
ISBN: 978-1-62937-389-8
Design by Amy Carter

CONTENTS

FOREWORDS *by Mike Krukow and Brandon Crawford*   v

INTRODUCTION   xi

CHAPTER 1: Giants DNA   1

CHAPTER 2: The Man   19

CHAPTER 3: 2010   39

CHAPTER 4: The Cleanup Spot   61

CHAPTER 5: Barry   105

CHAPTER 6: 2012   117

CHAPTER 7: Candlestick   133

CHAPTER 8: His Magnificence   145

CHAPTER 9: 2014   159

CHAPTER 10: No-Hitters   173

CHAPTER 11: The Nicest Man   183

AFTERWORD   193

ABOUT THE AUTHOR   201

APPENDIX   203

FOREWORDS

The weight of a Giants uniform is real. It has 134 years of history woven into it. It is a uniform that comes with expectation and accountability. Think about it: when you put on that uniform, you're connected with John McGraw, the "Little Napoleon" who managed the Giants to 10 National League pennants and three World Series titles. You're linked to Christy Mathewson, Bill Terry, Mel Ott, Carl Hubbell, and all the outstanding players from the franchise's tenure in New York.

And, of course, you're sustaining the tradition that seems to deepen every year since the franchise moved to San Francisco in 1958. You're representing the legacy of Willie Mays, Willie McCovey, Juan Marichal, Orlando Cepeda, and Gaylord Perry. As Brian Sabean, the architect of so many winning Giants ballclubs, has said, "They're not just statues." Yes, the greatness of those five Hall of Famers is captured in bronze outside of AT&T Park. But their names alone evoke what it means to be a Giant.

Look at the success this organization has had in the last 30 years. There's an expectation. You get that expectation only if you've had success. It wasn't always that way. But the job that Roger Craig and Al Rosen did to bring back pride when they came aboard at the end of the 1985 season was one of the most incredible things we ever witnessed. We saw the fan base come back in record numbers—it was cool to be a Giants fan again—and the guys who played in the 1950s and '60s came back as well. Mays and McCovey rejoined the team as special assistants. That was so cool, too. Cepeda, one of the brightest stars on the inaugural San Francisco team of 1958, appeared frequently at home games. All of a sudden, the Giants meant something again.

And then there was Will Clark. He was the catalyst of what was the renaissance and the resurgence of the organization, from top to bottom. When the team changed hands in 1993 and went to Peter Magowan and the new investors, that was the step that really solidified the resurgence.

Look at the type of players the Giants started drafting. You have to think there are other guys who maybe have more athletic talent, who

vi

might dazzle you a little more in batting practice or a home-run derby contest. But more and more Giants are coming up out of the minor leagues with a high baseball IQ. These guys can adjust to the speed of the big-league game and rely on instinct. It has become the Giants brand. It's the instinct of the first step on defense. It's the instinct of the first step on the base paths. To a degree, you can't teach that. You have to learn it by playing and do it through anticipation and intelligence.

Throughout a history that has spanned the country from New York to San Francisco, the team has been enriched by its relationship between the fans and players. It is what makes being a Giant special.

Nowadays, the Giants brand is established. For example, the Yankees have had off years. But they're still the Yankees because of what they've established historically. The Giants are the same kind of organization.

It is especially important that the Giants' history and their relationship with their fans is reported and recorded accurately. That task in itself comes with enormous responsibility. In the tradition of Leonard Koppett and Nick Peters, Chris Haft has taken on the task of preserving the memories that make up the Good Book San Francisco Giants. Haft has spent a career following the great game of baseball, and I once asked him if he ever played in the big leagues. Though he never played beyond high school, I told him that he writes as if he performed in the majors for 15 years. His passion is unequaled. He has written this book in a very entertaining and wonderful way, and I encourage you to savor it with the same attitude you would have if you were sitting down to watch a Sunday ballgame with your closest friend. Chris will make sure you have a great seat.

Enjoy!

—*Mike Krukow*

Mike Krukow is a seven-time Emmy-Award winning broadcaster and color commentator for the San Francisco Giants. He pitched for the Giants from 1983 to 1989.

It almost seemed like I was destined to be where I am now. My earliest baseball memories are of going to Giants games at Candlestick. My dad is a big fan, and he brought me to games when I was a baby. Months old. When I was a kid, I enjoyed mostly just being there. I might have gone down the Coke bottle slide at AT&T Park once.

Recently my dad was going through some old stuff of mine. I think it was from kindergarten, when we practiced handwriting and wrote about what we wanted to do upon growing up. I wrote that I wanted to be a professional baseball player.

And I certainly wanted to be a shortstop. It was always my favorite position. I think my first tee-ball card actually said "catcher," but I think that was more my dad than me. "The fastest way to the big leagues is as a switch-hitting catcher," is what he always said. And I switch-hit in tee-ball. But, yeah, I always liked shortstop the most. To be able to use some athleticism, use your arm and be in the middle of a lot of action, I like that.

There were a lot of guys who inspired me when I was really young. It's actually hard to narrow down. I definitely liked Royce Clayton, the Giants' shortstop. Right after that, I think it might have been A-Rod. A lot of people may not like to hear that nowadays, especially Giants fans. What am I doing rooting for a Seattle Mariner? But I think he became my favorite player because he was the first baseball card that I bought with my own money. I went to a card show with my dad. He used to take me to those things all the time to get some autographs and memorabilia, stuff like that, and I bought a card. I want to say it was 50 cents or less, because I didn't have a whole lot of money when I was eight years old. It happened to be Alex Rodriguez. So he became my favorite player through a baseball card at a card show. He ended up being pretty good also, so that's probably why I stuck with him.

What's special about playing for my hometown team? It's a hard question to answer because I don't know anything else. The Giants are the only team I've played for. Look at somebody like Joc Pederson, who grew up in the Bay Area. It's probably special to him to play for the Dodgers, because he's in the major leagues, even though he probably wasn't a big Dodgers fan growing up. Obviously I love playing for the Giants and I'd like to be with them my entire career. I did think about my connection to the team a little more when I first got called up in 2011, then when we won the World Series in 2012 and 2014. Being a Giant really was my dream growing up as a kid, and then winning a couple of World Series is even more than I ever dreamed of. I think that kind of puts it in perspective a little bit and makes me think about how lucky and fortunate I am to be in this position. Every year, we'll keep trying to make new memories for you that are as good as those described in these pages.

—*Brandon Crawford*

Brandon Crawford became the Giants' everyday shortstop in 2012. He won back-to-back Gold Glove awards for defensive excellence in 2015 and 2016 and was named a Silver Slugger recipient as the National League's top offensive performer at his position in 2015.

INTRODUCTION

Football was actually my first sports love. Through my Auntie Annabella I gained an appreciation for the Green Bay Packers, who were in the process of winning their second consecutive Super Bowl—pardon me, AFL-NFL Championship Game. Annabella took me to my first professional sporting event, a Packers–49ers game at San Francisco's Kezar Stadium in December 1968. During an unexpected stoppage in play, somebody yelled, "Must be time for a commercial," prompting laughter at this then-strange phenomenon. Postgame, I immediately joined the ranks of autograph hounds and managed to get the signatures of Bart Starr, Jerry Kramer, and Vince Lombardi, whose toothy grin remains fresh in memory. And when my schoolmates and I rushed out during recess to play "Kill the Pill," whichever star-crossed soul happened to be carrying the football (thus eligible to be tackled by anybody and everybody, hence the game's name) tried to emulate O.J. Simpson, for whom we reserved our highest praise. In the parlance of the day, O.J. was *bad*, completely without irony.

The third AFL-NFL Championship Game—uh, Super Bowl III— was the first televised sporting event I can remember watching from start to finish. Joe Namath was *bad*. Though the game's final gun briefly made me a sports orphan, I migrated easily to basketball. A hoop went up in the Haft driveway. Rarely would I be bored. Before sports began gripping me 24/7/365, playing "war" was my recreational passion. Then Martin Luther King and Bobby Kennedy got shot, and Dad revoked my Second Amendment rights by relieving me of my toy guns—which, in retrospect, looked more real than phony. "There's enough violence in the world without you adding to it!" he roared as he ripped a tommy gun from my grasp.

When spring came and my fourth-grade chums broke out bats and gloves, I was left behind. I wanted to keep up with the guys, but I lacked baseball equipment. Obviously favoring my wielding a bat instead of replica Lugers, Dad immediately brought home a black, 29-inch Ernie Banks model from the sporting goods store. Who was Ernie Banks? Why was my bat black and everybody else's was pale? I had a little trouble understanding baseball right away. I wanted more "Kill the Pill," but it was April and everybody was into baseball. So, completely incapable of swinging a bat or using a glove, I followed everybody to the sandlot at recess to participate in my first pickup game. One of the big sixth graders (I'm telling you, they seemed like adults) performed the role of manager and assigned me to the position universally reserved for novices: right field. Most kids were right-handed-batting pull hitters, so right fielders were seldom tested defensively. Thoroughly unaware of where I was supposed to go, I dutifully ran toward left field. "No, Chris—*right* field," said my skipper. He slowly shook his head as I changed course.

The Giants launched a long winning streak shortly after the 1969 season opened, prompting me to decide that I had better educate myself about this baseball stuff or else I'd have nothing in common with the guys. With the winning streak at eight games and the Dodgers coming into town, there was no better time to jump on the bandwagon. I fiddled with the tuning on my transistor radio, searching for KSFO-AM 560, then the Giants' all-powerful flagship station. But I kept getting what sounded like static. Soon I heard a voice that I'd come to know better than my own (this applied equally to Russ Hodges and Lon Simmons) saying, "I don't think that's Alston." I came to realize that the static was crowd noise and the man who wasn't Dodgers manager Walter Alston was their pitching coach, Red Adams, making a trip to the mound.

People who dislike baseball typically disparage it as being too slow. My feeling as I glued my radio to my ear was, *Are you kidding? The crowd was that jacked up when nothing was happening?! This is for me!* Within a couple of months I had checked out and read every baseball book on the shelves of the Menlo Park Public Library. I couldn't play the game worth a hoot, but it captivated me nonetheless.

Forty-seven years later, nothing's changed. I'm exceedingly fortunate to have made my passion my profession. A cynic might say that's a fancy way of describing myself as a homer. My response to that would be to shrug and resume assembling my next story. The various approaches I've taken to my job since I "turned pro" in July 1981 at the Twin Falls (Idaho) *Times–News* seem to have worked.

The jobs I've had and the ballgames I've seen, whether I witnessed them by purchasing a ticket or using a press pass, led to this book. Some of it is historical recitation, but it's not meant to be a compendium of the Giants' existence in San Francisco. People like reading about people, so wherever possible I tried to take an anecdotal look at ballplayers and events, with a particular emphasis on the "Giants DNA" concept that's highlighted in chapter 1.

I tried to conduct as many fresh interviews as possible, though I frequently relied on my personal archive of Giants stories. While I probed (with limited success) for the feeling of what it was like to be present during Edgar Renteria's impassioned speech to his teammates at Wrigley Field in September 2010, there was no point in asking Willie McCovey for the third time about Willie Mays' extreme nausea after devouring a plate of ribs the night before he hit four home runs in Milwaukee.

My favorite interview among the freshly minted ones might have been the briefest. Dennis Eckersley was a succinct, sheer delight as he shared his boyhood love for all things Giants, from announcers Russ and Lon to heroes Mays and Juan Marichal. Like many of us, Eckersley smuggled his radio into bed to listen to as many innings of night games as possible. "I used to keep stats on Marichal because he had some incredible seasons," Eckersley said. "I think I was up that night that he went 16 innings against Warren Spahn. I listened to that *frickin'* game." That's the kind of stuff I was looking for from Eckersley, who used a much saltier adjective than the one that's italicized, and others I approached.

This compilation is far from complete. Since it's weighted toward personal experiences as a reporter and observer, significant figures such as Orlando Cepeda, Jack Clark, and Matt Williams, events such as the 1962 World Series or the 1987 postseason, and the franchise's entire New York existence received little or no attention. In no way did I mean to convey a lack of regard or respect for any element of the Giants that was overlooked in the following pages. I simply lacked the where-withal—usually time or opportunities to conduct certain interviews—to include everything.

Then again, I tried to minimize the number of stones left unturned. Besides Mike Murphy, I might be the only person to have witnessed, in person, Marichal's and Gaylord Perry's final victories as Giants and Matt Cain's and Tim Lincecum's first. I aimed to convey at least some of this breadth.

Yes, this is a tad heavy on the late 1960s/early '70s. That's when I was introduced to baseball, and I suppose I'm an example of what author Kevin Nelson meant when he said, "The greatest era of baseball is the one you grew up with." Though I strive to keep this bias out of my current coverage, I do maintain a weakness for the complete game—so seldom seen nowadays. I can't help it that I saw Mike McCormick record one in the first Giants game I attended (San Francisco 5, Pittsburgh 2, May 24, 1969).

This wasn't meant to be the *Encyclopedia Britannica*, Giants-style. The people at Triumph Books were thoughtful enough to recognize my background and consider me capable of contributing to their If These Walls Could Talk series. Without either of us knowing that this series existed, this actually was a project that my friend and high school class-mate Robert Richmond suggested I undertake after one of the Giants' World Series triumphs. Rob, our late friend Bob Campbell, and I witnessed more than a few memorable games together at Candlestick Park. Usually they were Giants-Dodgers affairs, featuring Los Angeles' clinching the National League West in 1977; Mike Ivie's pinch-hit grand slam in May 1978; and McCovey's walkoff pinch-hit double in June 1980 which he hit days after announcing his impending retirement.

Aware of my experiences and tracing the path that the Giants had led me along, from nights at a near-deserted Candlestick to days teeming with thrills at AT&T Park, Rob urged me to put everything together in a book. I quickly dismissed the idea. "Who cares what I think?" I asked him, not caring what he thought of my reaction. Rob just kept smiling, repeating that I should do it. Of course, he was right—just like he was right when, as a painfully shy 20-year-old, I said that I'd never take a girl to a ballgame on a date. Said the omniscient Rob, "But Chris, that's exactly what you should do! Then she'll learn all about you!" At the time, maybe that's what I was afraid of.

That's enough self-psychoanalysis, though the Giants were responsible for an experience that truly was surreal—which has become an overused word, particularly in locker rooms and clubhouses where a synonym for unbelievable is being sought by players conducting interviews. But *surreal* summed it up on the afternoon when the Giants unveiled their Wall of Fame outside AT&T Park on September 23, 2008, honoring players who had spent at least nine years with the club or five years with at least one All-Star appearance. Shortly before the ceremony began, I walked through a hallway where the inaugural Wall class waited, standing roughly in chronological order of their Giants tenure. A few paces was all it took for me to sense that my entire Giants-related life was unfolding with each step. Bob Bolin...Jim

Davenport...Darrell Evans...Kevin Mitchell...J.T. Snow. They all smiled as I strode by. It was just the weirdest thing.

And it all began, really, with that first game at Candlestick. I immediately grew attached to the style of public-address announcer Jeff Carter, who combined showmanship with simplicity as he added a syllable to certain names ("Batter number 16, Jimmy Ray a-Hart!"). I remember being fascinated by that grand old scoreboard in right field, with all its numbers and abbreviations and advertisements. R? H? E? Longines—"official watch?" When's Willie Mays up again? Around the fourth or fifth inning, Dad used his gentle yet pointed tone to issue the words I would live by:

"Don't watch the scoreboard. Watch the game."

CHAPTER 1
GIANTS DNA

The early-arriving fans at the San Francisco Giants' 2016 home opener may not have realized it, but they were about to witness what amounted to a tribal ceremony—partly a rite of passage, partly an affirmation of family. The passage involved the journey from life to death; the family was a blended one, mixing members linked by blood as well as shared experience.

Jim Davenport, who played more games at third base than anybody in franchise history during a 13-year career spent with the Giants— *only* with the Giants—had died less than two months earlier, on February 18 at age 82. The ballclub had just begun spring training at Scottsdale, Arizona. There, word spread quickly of Davenport's death. I learned the news through a Giants coach. "We lost Davvy," he said simply. So, for the first time since—well, since virtually forever, in the Giants' San Francisco history—we wouldn't see Davenport instructing the club's younger prospects at minor league camp. Nor would we see Davenport bound into the major league clubhouse during one of his occasional visits, encouraging one of his protégés or saying hello to Willie Mays, his illustrious former teammate who for years has frequently appeared in the clubhouse, whether the team's in Scottsdale or San Francisco. Sometimes, Davenport brought Mays a baseball to autograph for a friend. Other times, they'd discuss their mutual roots in Alabama. Every time, it was a treat to see another legend on the premises. *Legend* is a word used too freely, but in the Giants' hierarchy of personalities, Jim Davenport was indeed a legend.

We lost Davvy. Exactly what, or who, had been lost? If you grew up in the San Francisco Bay Area during the 1960s, you knew the answer. Davenport was woven into the fabric of the Giants as tightly as the interlocking "SF" on the team's caps. While Mays, Willie McCovey, Juan Marichal, Orlando Cepeda, and Gaylord Perry have been honored with statues outside AT&T Park, the Giants' home, Davenport built his everlasting monument with the ballclub through the sheer length and breadth of his career. He worked within the organization for 51 years. Initially, he was the deft third baseman who broke into the major leagues in 1958, the franchise's inaugural season in San Francisco. As the club's primary leadoff hitter that year, Davenport was the first Giant to come to bat in the team's West Coast history. "Jimmy was one of those steadying rods on that team," McCovey said, referring collectively to the rosters that included Davenport. "Jimmy is as much a part of the Giant organization as me and Mays. We got all the publicity, but we all appreciated Jimmy. He looked up to guys like myself and Mays, but we looked up to him as much as he did us."

Davenport remained synonymous with the Giants not just because of his long playing career with them, but also because he and his family resided in San Carlos, a handful of home runs away from Candlestick Park (which needs no introduction). You might have encountered Davenport at the dedication of a baseball field or emerging from a local store. Or you may have almost literally bumped into him, as I did after playing in an interscholastic baseball or basketball game against one of his sons.

After retiring as a player in 1970, Davenport served the Giants as a coach and manager in the major and minor leagues, as well as in his final capacity as a roving instructor and special-assignment scout. "If you cut his veins, red wouldn't come out. It would be orange and black. I truly believe that," said Joe Amalfitano, another baseball "lifer" who was a kindred spirit of Davenport's. Hence the "tribal ceremony" conducted by the Giants, which included members of the Davenport family and select members of his baseball family—first baseman Brandon Belt, second baseman Joe Panik, shortstop Brandon Crawford, and third baseman Matt Duffy, who composed San Francisco's infield. It was a group the Giants were especially proud of, since it was composed exclusively of players drafted by the organization and developed within its system.

In the brief but meaningful ceremony, the Davenport clan and the Giants quartet planted third base into the infield dirt. The bag was emblazoned with the jersey No. 12 that Davenport wore during his playing career. One might imagine that this was a token appearance for the ballplayers, an obligation to dispense with as part of Opening Day, which is full of distractions. One would be wrong. If the Giants hadn't organized this tribute to Davenport, the infield foursome might have planned it on their own. Such was the esteem they reserved for Davenport and his son, Gary, who managed, coached, or instructed each of them during their apprenticeships in the Giants' farm system.

"All of us knew we had a game to play, but we weren't in a rush," Duffy said.

"We didn't really know what was expected of us for the ceremony, but we were like, 'We'll do whatever you guys want us to do.' Because Davvy was kind of like the folksy father figure to almost every minor leaguer in the organization. There was a huge level of respect and a lot of sad people when he passed."

"It was something I really wanted to be a part of," Belt said, referring to the ceremony. "Davvy and his whole family played an important role in me moving up in this organization."

When Davenport made his rounds at the minor league complex, he typically was joined by Amalfitano, another former infielder who's widely considered among the finest third-base coaches ever (never mind that he spent most of his career in the coaching box with the Dodgers). The infielders fondly recalled that Davenport and Amalfitano often supplemented their instruction of whatever fundamental they happened to be teaching by sharing an illustrative anecdote from a bygone ballgame. "It could be about a random game against the Cubs in the

Giants infielders Brandon Belt (9) and Brandon Crawford (35) join members of Jimmy Davenport's family during a pregame tribute to the longtime San Francisco third baseman at the 2016 home opener. Davenport was a roving instructor during his latter years with the organization and thus had a hand in the development of Belt, Crawford, and other homegrown Giants.

middle of May," Crawford said.

One way or another, the elders got their point across. Duffy cited a day when he was allowed to skip the afternoon's practice game, a privilege all minor leaguers receive after playing eight or nine days in a row. After participating in the morning workout, Duffy showered and headed for lunch, where he sat alongside Davenport and Amalfitano. They proceeded to feed Duffy extra helpings of baseball wisdom.

"I can't remember a specific story that they told, but we sat there talking for about two and a half hours. I stayed at the complex almost as long as the guys who were playing in the game that day," Duffy said. "I couldn't get myself to get up from the table because I was so entertained by Davvy and Joe telling old baseball stories. They were such unique people to me in a game that nowadays is very statistically and saber-metrically driven. When you have a moment like that, and you have the opportunity to just listen to them, you don't want those moments to end. Those are the guys you love to be around. Those are the guys you tell your kids about. Willie Mays is another of those guys I was so lucky to spend some time with and talk to briefly. Those are the guys who you remember, the guys who played the right way, played hard, taught hard.

"Those are the type of guys you want to grow up and be. There are guys who are role models who you can take things from, and then there's guys who make you think, 'If I end up like him when I'm that age, I will be so happy.' Because I just absolutely love those guys."

One way or another, Jim Davenport got his message across. Kevin Frandsen proved this. An infielder who grew up in San Jose rooting fiercely for the Giants, Frandsen was drafted by the organization in 2004 and sold to Boston during spring training in 2010. Despite leaving the Giants, he might as well have had Davenport's fundamentals tattooed on his forearm. For the remaining six years of his professional career, Frandsen continued to remind himself of Davenport's advice to crouch lower in his fielding stance as he played closer to home plate. "I think the reason the players liked him so much was he never talked down to them," Gary Davenport said. "He had that Southern charm and sense of humor."

Yet Jim Davenport could be as direct as a fastball when necessary. During Gary's tenure as hitting coach at Class A Advanced San Jose in 2009, concern rose regarding Conor Gillaspie, who was good enough to be selected 37th overall in the previous year's amateur draft. Gillaspie hit capably but defended awkwardly. Gary summoned his father, whose career was a testament to balanced skill. Davenport played 97 consecutive errorless games at third base from July 26, 1966, to April 28, 1968, a major league record at the time. He also was enough of an offensive threat to collect 10 game-winning hits in 1969, his final full season with the Giants. As Gary related, "Dad picks up his glove and said, 'Conor, you see this? If you don't learn to use this...'"—and with that he dropped the glove and brandished the nearest bat—"'...you'll never get to use this.'" (Gillaspie used his glove proficiently enough to receive most of the activity at third base with a week to go in the 2016 regular season after Eduardo Nunez injured his right hamstring. Gillaspie capitalized on the opportunity with a three-run, ninth-inning homer off Mets closer Jeurys Familia that accounted for all the scoring in the Wild Card Game. He proceeded to hit .400—6-for-15—in the Division Series against the eventual World Series–champion Chicago Cubs.)

The infielders spoke of the Davenports as if they were favorite teachers in school. Participating in the pregame ceremony, Panik said, "meant something because I had a relationship with both of those guys. Forget about baseball. Just the human being part of it. You won't find better men than those two."

While the players were at once graceful and gracious, Gary struggled with his composure. "I wasn't really sure what to expect that day. I mean, the emotions were over the top," he said. Seeing his father's grinning image on the Diamond Vision video board was overwhelming. Another manifestation of Jim, in a sense, was Panik, the Giants' current No. 12. Gary believed that Mike Murphy, the Giants' long-time clubhouse manager, made a solid choice by assigning the number to Panik when he was promoted to the majors in 2014. "You know, Murph doesn't just kind of haphazardly give out numbers," Gary said. "He wouldn't give Dad's number to anybody. To give it to Joe, I couldn't have picked a better person. Joe's very similar to Dad. He's got a lot of fire in him, he goes about his business, he's really quiet about it, he's just a grinder. He does all the little things that Dad taught in the minor leagues: hit-and-run, sacrifice bunt, bunt for hits."

Gary Davenport therefore had a final word reserved for Panik before the ceremony ended. Referring to the No. 12, Gary told Panik, "Wear it with pride." Panik would sooner take the field without his glove than do anything less. "That means something special," he said of perpetuating Davenport's legacy. "I take it seriously."

Gary knew this, but couldn't convey his sentiment to Panik. "When I told him that, I was so emotionally choked up that I didn't finish the sentence," Gary said.

"I wanted to finish by saying, 'Joe, you already have.'"

The morphing of Davenport into Panik is a prime example of what people in the club's organization like to call "Giants DNA"—the passion for competition, the diligence to prepare for it, and a sense of obligation to the fans that has passed from one generation of ballplayers to another, as if they were genetic traits.

Other teams share these qualities. But with the exception of a select few franchises, such as the Yankees, Dodgers, Red Sox, and Cardinals, none comes close to matching the Giants' star power. Baseball royalty runs in the Giants' blood. Theirs is an almost unbroken lineage of peerless performers dating back to the beginning of the game's modern era in 1900, when right-hander Christy Mathewson became the franchise's first true hero. Following him were Bill Terry, Carl Hubbell, Mel Ott, Willie Mays, Orlando Cepeda, Willie McCovey, Juan Marichal, Gaylord Perry, Bobby Bonds, Jack Clark, Vida Blue, Will Clark, Barry Bonds, Jeff Kent, Tim Lincecum, Buster Posey, and Madison Bumgarner. They were complemented by others who gained less fame but still inspired baseball dreams, such as Johnny Mize, Bobby Thomson, Monte Irvin, Sal Maglie, Jack Sanford, Billy Pierce, Stu Miller, Jim Ray Hart, Chris Speier, Gary Matthews, Garry

Maddox, John Montefusco, Darrell Evans, Jeffrey Leonard, Chili Davis, Bob Brenly, Robby Thompson, Dave Dravecky, Kevin Mitchell, Matt Williams, Rod Beck, Rich Aurilia, Robb Nen, Matt Cain, Pablo Sandoval, and Hunter Pence.

Club president Larry Baer, who regularly attended Giants games during boyhood and might still have traces of Candlestick Park hot dogs in his bloodstream, affirmed that Giants DNA is more than just a catchy phrase. "It's a serious, weighty, and full-of-gravitas notion that wearing a Giants uniform matters," he said. "It means something. It means something because it's connecting to generations past, generations past that were some of the icons of the sport, icons of the community. What Willie Mays meant to New York City when the Giants were there. What Willie McCovey, Barry Bonds, Madison Bumgarner, Buster Posey mean to this region as they're here. Putting on the Giants uniform is a big thing. It entails responsibility. What goes with it is more than a ballplayer coming through playing a game. The reason it has that responsibility is a baseball team is not just about winning baseball games. What it's about is the memory-making that goes on and the experiences with friends and family. It can be the background music of your life, being at the ballpark with people you care about, and your own experiences with that, touching family and friends and community."

This closeness often exists among the Giants themselves. Consider the bond between Davenport and Amalfitano, who were Giants teammates in 1960–61 and 1963. "Those two guys were inseparable," Duffy said. Sent from San Francisco to Tampa Bay at the 2016 Trade Deadline, Duffy observed that the environment within the Giants organization encourages relationships such as the one those seasoned pros forged.

"For all those guys to be such good friends for as long as they have, it really speaks to that the Giants didn't feel like an organization. It felt like a family," Duffy said. "It sounds so clichéd. But that stuff doesn't just happen. They work to make that happen. It also takes the willingness and the want of their alumni and current players to facilitate that atmosphere."

Brian Sabean, the architect of the Giants' trio of early-21st-century World Series winners, expressed respect for the ties linking all who possess Giants DNA. Sabean worked for the Yankees before joining the Giants in 1993; he was New York's vice president of player development and scouting director when Derek Jeter was drafted sixth overall in 1992. He insisted that for all the hallowed history that's woven into those pinstripes, the Giants manage and nurture their legacy more carefully than the Yankees do.

"This organization is so rooted in its past but so alive in its present," said Sabean, the Giants' longtime general manager who morphed into executive vice president of baseball operations in 2015. "Our history speaks for itself. I think it's more amazing for me, personally, having come from the Yankees, that I can honestly say that this bond here is so much stronger and so much on a day-to-day basis than even my Yankee experience."

Left-hander Jeremy Affeldt, who retired after the 2015 season and became a Giants television commentator the following year, delivered his stream-of-consciousness assessment of Giants history and its impact.

"Look at the stages in which this team is built. Not necessarily world championships. But the stages of guys," Affeldt said. "You have the Willie McCoveys, the Mayses, Gaylord Perry, you have all these old-school guys who built a pretty awesome team that everybody loved and did some phenomenal things.

"Then these guys stayed around the team and you get into the '80s and you have Dravecky and they set another stage and you have Bonds who set another stage and you have all these guys. Will the Thrill, man.

All these names who just did so many great things. And then all of a sudden you get the Timmys and the Cains and the [Brian] Wilsons and you've got the no-hitters and you've got Buster Posey and Madison Bumgarner—names that had high impact not just on the team but on the game of baseball." Here Affeldt cited Posey's and Bumgarner's brisk jersey sales following their respective World Series exploits.

Affeldt concluded, "The history of San Francisco expects you to come in and represent baseball correctly. Before you leave here, you're going to know how to win. And you're going to know what it means to expect to win."

It's not just the players with recognizable names and the World Series champs who matter. Remember John Tamargo and his Opening Day home run in 1979? Were you there the day Joe Pettini got four hits? And who can forget the Ron Pruitt game? Or the night in September 2010 when Darren Ford sped around the bases to score the winning run?

Don't misunderstand the Giants' priorities. The tireless baseball operations staff—which was back at work the day after San Francisco completed its seminal triumph in the 2010 World Series—remains squarely focused on the future, which is the only way to build a winner. However, the Giants also honor the past with sincerity and understand that bygone eras and individuals maintain a certain relevance. In the immortal words of William Faulkner, "The past is not dead. In fact, it's not even past." Which leads to Brandon Belt, Joe Panik, Brandon Crawford, and Matt Duffy helping honor Jim Davenport before the 2016 home opener.

Giants broadcaster Mike Krukow, who pitched for the team during one of its occasional lulls (1983–85) but stuck around for the renaissance, eloquently summarized what makes the Giants *the Giants*.

"There's a weight when you put that uniform on," Krukow said, insisting that one can almost feel each year of the franchise's history envelop him along with the jersey. He added, "I think that there's a responsibility. You're not just a player. You're a curator. The people who played before you established this franchise. You're keenly aware of that history when you put that uniform on for the first time and you're keenly aware of the rivalry you have with the Dodgers. So I think that there's a responsibility with this club that a lot of teams don't have. When you win here, there's such a deep feeling of respect from the fans that lasts well beyond the last game played that season. They don't forget you. And that's a humbling thing for an athlete."

The respect Krukow speaks of has been tested. Check the attendance figures. The years of embarrassingly small crowds, which began in the Mays-McCovey-Marichal era, could be traced to the downright inhospitable conditions at Candlestick. But if fans had a reason to rush to the ballpark, they'd respond. Before the 1978 season, the Giants traded seven players to the A's for Blue, who remained exceedingly popular. So did McCovey, who was brought back the previous season. Thus, the Giants' roster featured the Bay Area's two most popular big leaguers who were still active. Couple that with the most effective promotional commodity—winning—and watch the turnstiles spin. In a turnaround that was nothing short of stunning, Giants attendance soared from 700,056 in 1977 to 1,740,477 in '78. The next quantum leap occurred when the Peter Magowan–led group purchased the team and lured free-agent outfielder Barry Bonds to the Giants. After drawing 1,561,987 in 1992 and nearly relocating to Tampa–St. Petersburg, the Giants nearly doubled that to 2,606,354 in '93. That club, of course, won 103 games and featured Bonds' remarkable exploits.

The road had been paved for the move to AT&T Park, which was (and is) as fan-friendly as Candlestick was unpleasant. But as the new ballpark approached its 10th birthday, sellout crowds were the exception rather than the rule. The Giants franchise had given the club's fan base so much, but the patrons wanted still more. For me, of course, the Giants' mere existence was enough. At the same time, I'd lose all credibility in my role as MLB.com's Giants beat reporter if I functioned as an apologist for the organization. In a burst of writing that was as impassioned as it was brief, I called for more patience from the fans in my regular off-season question-and-answer column, though I understood their hunger for a World Series trophy. Here was how I responded to an exasperated fan who wanted reasons for continuing to support the team:

You stick with the Giants because that's just what fans do. Otherwise, you're something else beginning with the letter "f"—fickle. You stick with the Giants because you understand that baseball is a game of failure (remember, even the best hitters return to the dugout fruitlessly seven times every 10 at-bats) and only people who can't grasp what the game's about demand constant success. You stick with the Giants because hope is one of the biggest words in the English language, and because watching guys like Matt Cain, Fred Lewis, Randy Winn, Brian Wilson, and Pablo Sandoval give you hope. You stick with the Giants because Tim Lincecum pitches every five days, and there isn't a better show in baseball than that.

You stick with the Giants because they're among baseball's crown jewel franchises and they play in a gem of a ballpark. You stick with the Giants because you cherish the link to legends like Mathewson, Mays, Marichal, and Bonds (pick either one). You stick with the Giants because, if you're around 40 or older, you saw them almost move to Toronto and Denver and Tampa-St. Petersburg, so now you'll never let them go. You stick with the Giants because you feel like your scalp would break out in a rash if you put on a different team's cap. Go ahead and switch to the A's or Dodgers or Phillies; life is full of many more important choices. If it's that easy to jump ship, you never were a true fan anyway.

Those three World Series titles, along with genuine mutual warmth between players and fans, have cemented the team's popularity. Players truly feel the love washing over them from the stands.

Ask Ryan Vogelsong, the right-hander whose precipitous fall from major league life and subsequent rise to All-Star status captivated fans.

"It's a special place because the fans are different. They're not just fans. There's a relationship there with their team," said Vogelsong, San Francisco's leading winner in the 2012 postseason. "They genuinely care about their guys. They're not just showing up to yell at you or boo you. They genuinely care about the player and what's going on with him."

That was apparent on May 8, 2011, after Vogelsong made the first AT&T Park start of his Giants renaissance. San Francisco drafted him in the fifth round in 1998 before trading him to Pittsburgh with outfielder Armando Rios on July 30, 2001, for right-hander Jason Schmidt and pinch-hitter John Vander Wal. Vogelsong then pitched in Japan from 2007 to '09 and divided 2010 between the Angels' and Phillies' Triple-A affiliates. He signed a minor league contract on January 14, 2011, with the Giants, who actually offered less money than the Dodgers. Leaving the game with one out in the seventh inning and a 3–0 lead, Vogelsong received a warm, appreciative ovation. After he doffed his cap to reciprocate the fans' sentiment, they cheered even louder.

No wonder that after the 2015 season finale, Vogelsong spoke on the public-address system to thank the fans and deliver a personal message. Though it was obvious that he'd head elsewhere in free agency,

Vogelsong said memorably, "I will always, always, be a Giant." When Vogelsong visited San Francisco as a member of the Pittsburgh Pirates on August 15, 2016, he soaked in a pregame ovation before pitching that night. When he left the game after 5⅔ innings, fans again increased the volume of their cheering for Vogelsong, behind whom San Francisco won all seven of his postseason starts in 2012 and 2014. Clearly moved by the reaction, Vogelsong doffed his cap once more.

"I'm out there in the right-field corner (warming up before the game), and the fans are screaming at me, and I love every second of it," said Vogelsong, who acknowledged that dwelling on this start beforehand had exhausted him.

In a sense, it always been this way inside AT&T Park. It's just that there are more fans around now, and players give them more opportunities to cheer.

Left-hander Kirk Rueter never played on a World Series–winning team, though he came excruciatingly close in 2002. A Giant from 1996 to 2005, Rueter derived his greatest pleasure from his interaction with fans and the excitement they amplified. "That was the most special thing for me," Rueter said. "Granted, I loved winning and we had a lot of great teams, which makes it a lot better. But I loved being around the people and having fun with them. Fans will forget the good games and the bad games, but hopefully they won't forget what kind of person and player you were when you were here."

Other prominent Giants felt the love and shall always cherish it. Beneath Jeff Kent's flinty exterior, for example, was a profound regard for the fans.

"As cold as it was, as aggravating as it can be for games, the fans showed up," said Kent, who won the 2000 National League Most Valuable Player award with the Giants. "They were loud, they disliked the opposing teams; I think that's all great. The fans made the experience for me."

15

Another MVP, slugging left fielder Kevin Mitchell (1989), echoed Kent. "If it wasn't for the fans, we wouldn't be who we are," Mitchell said. "The fans made me a ballplayer. They kept me to where I wanted to play for that city and that organization. They treated me first-class. It was an honor to play for that city."

For Darrell Evans, the classy third baseman, the seeds of curiosity about Giants fans were planted when he was growing up in southern California during the 1960s. "The only games we got to watch on television were the Game of the Week and the Giants–Dodgers games," Evans recalled. "I remember watching people at Candlestick wearing their parkas in June or July and you think, 'What the heck's going on? Man, they've got to be the greatest fans in the world.' And it turned out they were."

J.T. Snow reveled in the sheer vibe at Candlestick. When he joined the Giants in 1997, he understood instantly that because the conditions were so miserable, the people who showed up *really* wanted to be there. "There might be 10,000 people in the stands on a Tuesday night against the Montreal Expos, and it's cold, but they were loud and they were into it," said the slick-fielding first baseman. "I enjoyed it, because they let you know when you're doing well and they let you know when you're not doing well. As a player, you like that. To me, it's an East Coast city with East Coast fans, just not to the extreme of Boston or New York or Philadelphia."

It follows that those who share Giants DNA are part of a family. You saw how closely knit the family is when Lincecum learned that he had won his first Cy Young Award, dropped by the clubhouse, and received a warm embrace from Mays, the patriarch. You hear about it when a new player joins the team and tells reporters that he fielded phone calls from the likes of Posey, Cain, or manager Bruce Bochy welcoming him to the club within hours, sometimes minutes, of his acquisition. You see it whenever superstar-turned-instructor Will Clark, ever the dual threat, joins the team at spring training or during the regular season and shares his considerable knowledge about hitting or fielding—sometimes quiet and intent, sometimes noisy and teasing, but always well-meaning. We see it before the final Friday home game of each regular season, when the "Willie Mac" Award is presented to that year's most inspirational player—and, invariably, numerous former winners attend the festivities out of sheer respect. I encountered it in the catacombs of Cincinnati's Riverfront Stadium, when I covered the Reds, and I happened upon hitting coach Bobby Bonds inspecting Robby Thompson's swing as he swatted baseballs into a net. They glanced at me for a nanosecond and returned to their craft, but not before I took a mental picture of the scene and titled it "Last Vestiges of Giant Pride," acknowledging not only the august individuals but also the team's struggling status at the time.

Given the oft-cyclical nature of a professional sports team's fortunes, the Giants probably will endure hard times again. But when they do, that DNA may enable them to recover more quickly than other teams might. Ask Frandsen. A San Jose native, Frandsen grew up rooting feverishly for the Giants and was overjoyed when they made him their 12th-round selection in the 2004 draft out of San Jose State University. During his tenure in the Giants' farm system and while playing in the minors with five other organizations, he was disappointed to find that a large number of minor leaguers couldn't care less about the team concept. When he rejoined the Giants as part of Triple-A Sacramento's roster in 2015, he stumbled upon a team with attitude—the right attitude.

"A lot of guys in the minor leagues are so jealous of everything and so worried about who's ahead of them, who wasn't, what the moves were," Frandsen said. "Last year I experienced something with the

Giants that I never have in the minor leagues, and I know it's been going on for a while—the fact that guys were in it for each other. They were about winning, about learning. Ninety percent of them. I would never say it was toxic, but when I was coming up, it almost felt like it was every man for himself. I'm not using it as an excuse, but you can understand why I got frustrated. It's because that was the culture that was around. I feel like success breeds success, but also success breeds good character. I feel like the success that the major league club had filtered all the way down and guys understood that it was about preparing, it was about that night, it was about that game, not about what you can't control."

Regardless of what course the franchise takes, one man remains the embodiment of its greatness. He's a true American original who captured the imagination of millions years ago and will forever represent the best that baseball and the Giants have to offer.

CHAPTER 2
THE MAN

Baseball turned me into a backseat driver between the ages of 10 and 12. On those special handful of days when my parents and I visited Candlestick Park, upon arriving there I urged Dad to wind his way into a parking spot that was as close as possible to the players' parking lot. Once Dad shut off the car's motor, mine was racing as I sprinted to the wire fence enclosing the players' lot. All I looked for was one automobile—a shiny, sleek pink Cadillac. That's what Willie Mays drove. Crossing the turnstiles was secondary to knowing that The Man was on the premises. Like thousands of other boys around the country, I was under Willie's spell.

Introducing the American statesman Adlai Stevenson here might seem kind of odd. Like Mays, Stevenson was a prominent national figure in the 1950s, though Dwight D. Eisenhower swept him in a doubleheader of presidential elections in 1952 and '56. What possible connection might Adlai Stevenson have with Willie Mays? Consider this oft-repeated quotation of Stevenson's, which is favored by speakers at college graduations (as it was at mine): "Your days are short here; this is the last of your springs. And now in the serenity and quiet of this lovely place, touch the depths of truth, feel the hem of Heaven. You will go away with old, good friends. *And don't forget when you leave why you came.*"

Willie Howard Mays was why so many of us came to baseball—glove in one hand, bat in the other, swinging with abandon and chasing distant fly balls in the hope that we could do either with a fraction of his grace and panache. He was synonymous with excellence, and we firmly believed that he could do anything. That's why, for me, no season opener ever will top my first on April 7, 1970, when the Giants faced the Houston Astros at Candlestick. I don't recall ordering Dad where to park that day; I'm sure I remained on my best behavior because my parents actually obtained permission for me to skip school. It began as an afternoon full of wonder. I knew nothing of Opening Day's pageantry, so I was in awe of the banners and bunting that brightened Candlestick's concrete facades. I was thrilled to see and hear Russ Hodges, the avuncular Giants broadcaster, stand at home plate with a microphone and deliver his signature greeting, "How ya' doin' everybody?" I didn't realize that players would trot to the baselines as Hodges introduced them individually. All this was traditional, but it was new to me. I reveled in it.

Again, I thought Willie could do anything. When he smashed a first-inning RBI single, I was convinced that this would be the greatest afternoon of my life. Eight innings remained; who knew what other feats he might perform? Willie got another base hit in his next plate appearance, inspiring me to proclaim to anybody who would listen, "He's gonna bat 1.000 this year!" I seem to remember that a couple of adults chuckled at my mingled exuberance and ignorance. In fact, Willie went hitless in his next three plate appearances, so by the end of the game I reluctantly accepted reality and downgraded my 1970 projection for him. *He'll win the batting title*, I concluded.

On the 15 or so occasions when I was fortunate enough to see Mays play, I knew that I should abandon any pursuit of hot dogs, popcorn, or autographs and return to my seat about 10 minutes before the scheduled first pitch. That's when Mays, alone, would emerge from the dugout and warm up by playing catch with one of the batboys, whom I considered the luckiest kid in the Bay Area.

The Bible urges us to put away childish things as adults. I'm not sure whether my fascination with Willie Mays was childish. I do know that I couldn't put it away. If anything, it grew through the years, as my perspective on baseball changed. The longer I covered baseball, the more I appreciated Willie, for I realized how superior he was to virtually everyone else. I read that he should have won the NL Most

Valuable Player awards in 1962 and '64, which would have doubled his career haul. Legend has it that he would intentionally swing and miss in relatively harmless situations, just so the unsuspecting hurler might throw him the same pitch later in the game with men on base—*pow*. Joe Amalfitano wouldn't confirm this for me, but he did recall watching Mays foul off a pitch and complain about the stinging in his hands, known far and wide as the "bees in the bat handle" that flee their hive when a hitter makes lousy contact. The enterprising hurler thought he'd repeat the pitch. *Wham*. Somewhere, it's still going.

Mays' skills had begun declining by the time I discovered baseball. It didn't matter. I saw him hit a home run; Baseball-reference.com reminded me that this great event occurred on May 30, 1971, in the first game of a doubleheader off Montreal Expos ace Bill Stoneman. What I remember without any online prompting was that the Candlestick grounds crew later dug up home plate to give it to Mays. The homer was his 1,950[th] run scored, breaking Stan Musial's National League record. At the time, league marks were still a huge deal. I was impressed not just by Mays' latest accomplishment but also with the grounds crew's grave, meticulous handling of the plate, as if they were unearthing a dinosaur's pelvic bone.

Slightly less than a month later I watched Mays strike out four times in four at-bats against the Padres. Certainly, I was disappointed, but if you think that Mays' performance soured me on him in any way, you haven't been paying attention. *He* wasn't down on himself at all. If anything, it almost looked as if he were strutting back to the dugout after each out. His elegant body language seemed to say, *Yeah, I struck out, but I'm still Willie Mays.*

Later that summer I was treated to seeing Willie Mays at his very best. This Friday, August 13, affair against the New York Mets wasn't a must-win situation, but it was one of those games over the course of a

Every boy, it seemed, who grew up in the San Francisco Bay Area during the 1960s wanted to be Willie Mays. One of those youths was Dennis Eckersley, raised in the suburb of Fremont. "Mays was the man," said Eckersley, the future Cy Young Award winner.

long season that a team needed to capture to avoid starting or extending a slump. The Giants had lost eight of their previous 10 games and their once-enormous NL West lead had dwindled to 3½ games over the Dodgers. Fortunately for the Giants, Mays took care of everything.

Ex-Giant Ray Sadecki started for the Mets and struck out the first two batters. Up came Mays, who smoked a line drive up the middle for a single that almost decapitated Sadecki. *You're not getting past me,* was my interpretation of Mays' subliminal message. *This is* my *game.*

Mays proceeded to add an RBI double and a triple in his next two at-bats. He scored both times, stealing third base following the double to come home on a sacrifice fly. Oh, and he made a nice play or two in center field. I was furious with Giants manager Charlie Fox when he removed Mays from the game in the seventh inning. I felt certain that Mays would belt a home run and hit for the cycle. It didn't occur to me that Fox wanted to keep the 40-year-old Mays fresh for the next day's game.

It was suggested that Willie would intentionally make a play more difficult than it looked to create suspense for the fans. For instance, he might slow down on the base paths to slide in barely ahead of the throw, or delay his pursuit of a batted ball ever so slightly so he would reach it just in time. This sounds a trifle risky, but it makes me wonder whether he staged this little scene I witnessed one night at Candlestick: He dropped an inning-ending pop fly, then snatched the ball inches from the turf before it fell safely. I wouldn't be surprised if he did it to give us all a little thrill.

In my reporter's guise, I was fortunate enough to talk to Willie several times. One of my favorite conversations was the shortest. I asked him one afternoon at spring training, "How did you stay in great shape?" He smiled, stood a tad straighter, puffed out his chest ever so slightly, and replied, "I never got *out* of shape." Common-sense wisdom at its finest. Remember, the man played before personal trainers were all the rage. He remained 5'11", 180 pounds from one Opening Day to the next.

I'm far from alone in my fascination regarding Mays. He was the subject of not one, not two, but three full-length television documentaries: *A Man Named Mays* (1963), *Portrait of Willie Mays* (1967), and *A New Ball Game for Willie Mays* (1974). Except for Jackie Robinson and the hallowed Yankees trio of Babe Ruth, Joe DiMaggio, and Mickey Mantle, probably no other ballplayer has drawn as much attention.

Even in his retirement, as was the case when he played, you couldn't take your eyes off him. Otherwise, you might miss him doing something memorable. In spring training 2016, infielder Ryder Jones, a nonroster invitee whom the Giants selected in the second round of the 2013 draft, approached Mays and asked him to appraise one of his bats. "It ain't the bat," Willie said. He grabbed the bat near the label and flicked his wrist. "You've gotta have that *snap*," he said, as the barrel of the bat cut through the air like a fencer's epee.

Countless youths of various generations shared my fanaticism. One was Richard Francis Dennis Barry, known to the world as Rick Barry, the pro basketball Hall of Fame forward. As a kid, I came to adore Barry almost as much as I worshiped Willie, but that's another story. Barry grew up in Roselle Park, New Jersey, about 20 miles from New York. The Giants and Dodgers hadn't yet moved west, so they were still vying annually with the Yankees for local baseball supremacy. Most kids picked a favorite team among the three and doggedly stuck by it. For Barry, it was the Giants. "I didn't like the Dodgers, and I was a Yankee-hater growing up," said Barry, who was enamored of baseball before he began concentrating on basketball in high school.

Barry's father had taught him a method of snaring fly balls that looked unusual but allowed the fielder to release throws quickly. It was the basket catch. And at about that time, Barry's beloved Giants called up a center fielder who essentially made the basket catch his signature.

"So that was my guy from that point on," Barry said, referring to Mays. "He was a pretty good choice."

Barry continued to adore Mays as an adult. It just so happened that he started his NBA career with the San Francisco Warriors, enabling him to earn a place with Mays in the Bay Area's athletic pantheon. Because he identified so closely with Mays, Barry wore his hero's jersey number—24. That remained constant for Barry until he signed with the Houston Rockets as a free agent before the 1978–79 season. No. 24 on the Rockets belonged to star center Moses Malone, who wasn't inclined to yield his number. However, nothing would stop Barry from continuing to pay homage to Mays. He simply wore No. 2 at home and No. 4 on the road.

Through the years, Mays and Barry crossed paths on multiple occasions. Barry remains eternally grateful. "I mean, think about this," he said. "I became friends with my boyhood athletic hero. It's unbelievable."

Another Hall of Famer, right-hander Dennis Eckersley, began his association with baseball as a rabid Giants fan reared in Fremont, about 40 miles southeast of San Francisco.

"I *loved* the Giants," Eckersley said. "Everything was the Giants. That's where my passion began. I loved Lon Simmons and Russ Hodges, man. Big time. I loved Juan Marichal.

"Obviously," Eckersley added, "Mays was the man."

He was singular because he was not just talented, but also driven; because he was not only accomplished, but also charismatic; because his skills were not merely pronounced, but also diverse.

For instance, the basket catch was more than different. It was also sensible, as young Rick Barry learned. Additionally, Mays didn't always display classic hitting form. Sometimes he seemed to leap at the ball, defying the fundamental approach of keeping one's head still. But when he sent pitches hurtling over the wall or into the gaps, whether he followed proper hitting technique didn't really matter.

In a 2008 interview, Mays gave me a look behind his showmanship and excellence.

"I would go home at night and create what I was going to do the next day," he said. "It sounds kind of childish. But if I feel that we're going to have a good crowd or something, and I want to do something the next day to make sure the crowd enjoyed what I did, well, then I'd look at a couple of films by myself and figure out something that I can do to make them holler. And I would do it."

Mays frequently realized these dreams, as numerous statistics indicate—3,283 hits, 2,062 runs, 660 homers, 1,903 RBIs, and a .302 batting average. One could add his 12 consecutive Gold Glove awards as a reflection of his defensive excellence. But that streak actually served as an inadequate measure of Mays' prowess afield, since the honor wasn't created until 1957, his fifth full season in the majors.

If any set of numbers reflect Mays' greatness, he forged them in 1969, when he became the first player to amass at least 300 home runs and 300 stolen bases. This cemented his long-established reputation as the quintessential combination of power and speed. Only the rarest players possess both qualities in abundance, besides being able to excel at all other facets of the game.

"I created my own identity," Mays said.

Ultimately, Mays' magic transcended statistics. Nobody expressed this better than his first major league manager, Hall of Famer Leo Durocher. Asked constantly about Mays, whom he nurtured through his first three full seasons, Durocher repeated the following almost verbatim on each occasion: "If somebody came up and hit .450, stole 100 bases and performed a miracle in the field every day, I'd look you in the eye and say Willie was better. He could do the five things you have to do to be a superstar: hit, hit for power, run, throw and field. And he had that other magic ingredient that turns a superstar into a super superstar. He lit up the room when he came in. He was a joy to be around."

Felipe Alou spoke almost mournfully of the tendency to reduce Mays and other greats to a clump of numbers. "It's too bad that when it comes to evaluating guys like Willie Mays, Hank Aaron and Barry Bonds, people only look at the home runs," said the estimable Alou, who played alongside the first two greats and managed the third. "People aren't interested in all of the other stuff that a guy like Willie, especially, could do. Speed and base-running expertise. Defense. It hurts me that the average fan doesn't know the real Willie Mays. They only read about 660 homers and the 'Say Hey Kid.' I know all of that is important, but the whole package of this tremendous player is lost."

However, there exists a stat with a touch of soul that summarizes Mays' enduring impact and avoids decimal points. According to figures provided by Pete Palmer, a writer and editor of various baseball publications, the Giants led the NL in road attendance nine times in 11 years between 1961 and 1971. Everybody wanted to see The Man. Said Alou, "Any city that we played in, when we arrived there, the newspaper said, 'Willie Mays and company.' In the 'company' was Juan Marichal, Gaylord Perry, Willie McCovey. Willie Mays was the big guy, no question about it. We knew that."

He prided himself in being more than a slugger. I recognized this personally late one afternoon in 2005, my initial season covering the Giants. Alou posted the lineup with the cleanup spot blank. Barry Bonds was on the disabled list. As I recall, a couple of other players were injured, accounting for the delay in finalizing the lineup while Alou searched for able-bodied men. Mays happened to be visiting the clubhouse. As he strode by, veteran San Francisco Chronicle reporter David Bush playfully asked him, "Hey, Willie, are you batting cleanup?" Initially, Mays declined to acknowledge the humor. "Naw, man," he said. However, some competitive ember must have smoldered within him, because he suddenly looked at us over his shoulder and offered this suggestion: "Leadoff."

Of course. Mays batted leadoff in eight All-Star Games, during the era when it remained a glamorous event. And no other All-Star was more glamorous than Mays, who shares the record for appearances in the Midsummer Classic with Stan Musial and Hank Aaron (24) and holds the marks for at-bats (75), runs (20), hits (24), and stolen bases (six). He and Musial also top the All-Star list with eight extra-base hits apiece. "We didn't play Interleague Games, and we didn't have the television exposure that they have now, so most of the people in the American League didn't get a chance to see the National League stars until the All-Star Game," McCovey said. "That's why Ted Williams made the statement that the All-Star Game was made for Willie Mays. He got to showcase his talents to the world."

In preparing a package of feature stories about Mays, I sought fresh insight without trying to get too intrusive or personal. I asked several of Mays' teammates to tell me what people should know about him that they might not already realize. The responses were unanimous: He was a superb team leader.

Marichal recalled that before his starts, he and Mays discussed how he planned to approach each hitter. Marichal called it the "three-minute meeting." Mays also conducted these strategy sessions with Gaylord Perry, San Francisco's only other starter who could be trusted to locate his pitches consistently. Marichal said that the Giants' starting catcher *du jour* participated in the meetings. But Mays countered, "No, man. We didn't need a catcher." By learning how each hitter would be pitched,

Mays could estimate where each ball would be hit. And he positioned the other outfielders accordingly. "He played the hitters so well," said Marichal, the Hall of Fame right-hander. "If you made a mistake, right away he'd come and tell you. 'You were supposed to pitch him away, and you threw a breaking ball, and he pulled the ball and got a hit.' That's *your* mistake. When you were on that mound, you tried not to make any kind of mistake. Otherwise you were going to hear from Willie."

And for good reason.

"I tell people this all the time: the pitcher is your key to playing outfield," Mays said. "If you know what he's going to do, I feel it's very easy to play. But you have to be on the same page. You know those balls hit in the gap? I'd catch a lot of those. Because I'd know how he's going to pitch."

Right-hander Bob Bolin saw Mays prevent countless runs while pitching for the Giants from 1961 to '69. "There'd be a line drive in the gap between right center or left center and you're thinking, 'Ohhhh, there goes the ballgame,' and there goes Mays up against the wall," Bolin said.

Outfielder Ken Henderson joined the Giants at age 18 due to the "bonus rule," which preceded the advent of the annual June draft and stipulated that an amateur signing for a bonus that exceeded a certain sum of money had to begin his professional career in the big leagues. This often stunted the development of talented but unpolished players such as Henderson, who were stuck at the end of the dugout bench when they really needed minor league seasoning. Fortunately for Henderson, he was nurtured by Mays. "I'll never forget as a rookie, Willie once told me that, to him, defense was the most important part of the game," Henderson said. "I found that really amazing for a guy who was such an outstanding hitter, base runner, you name it, he had all the skills. It kind of registered with me. I really bought into Willie's logic."

Minor league pitcher Jerry Thomas nicknamed Henderson "Skitch"—after Skitch Henderson, one of the bandleaders for *Tonight Show* host Johnny Carson. Hence Mays approached the novice Henderson and said, "'Skitch,' if you ever have any questions, don't hesitate to come to me.'" During an intrasquad game, Mays proved to Henderson that his paternal attitude was genuine. Playing center field for one team—Mays, of course, was in center for the other squad— Henderson dove for a sinking line drive that he had no chance of catching. Henderson's effort was futile but sincere. After all, he had a legend to emulate. *Defense is the most important part of the game.* He missed the ball by two feet and slammed into the ground so hard that he briefly knocked himself out. When Henderson came to his senses, he realized that Mays was the first person who had rushed to check on him. "It was an incident I'll never forget," Henderson said.

When infielder Hal Lanier was promoted to San Francisco in June 1964, he found Mays ready to help him.

"He took me by the hand and showed me the ins and outs of the major leagues," Lanier said. "During a game, he'd position me with different hitters. I'd look over my right shoulder and see him motioning me one way or another."

Seven years later, Chris Speier succeeded Lanier at shortstop and received similar treatment from Mays.

"If you asked him anything, he was always there to help you," Speier said. "He'd always talk about hitters and pitchers and how they'd try to intimidate you. He was always very, very supportive."

Other players, from Giants to rivals, reciprocated Mays' generous spirit with sheer idolatry. "He *was* baseball," said third baseman Al Gallagher, who in 1970 became the first native San Franciscan to play for the Giants. "To me, Willie was the greatest guy ever."

Bill White, former first baseman and National League president, spoke in tones as regal as a Shakespearean actor. Yet in discussing Mays, his words conveyed a little boy's love. "If there ever were a baseball god," White declared, "it would be he. Nobody could play like him. Nobody."

Like any deified figure, Mays' legend remains intact. He played his last game on October 16, 1973, in Game 3 of the World Series for the New York Mets against the Oakland A's. He was 42 and plainly past his prime. However, ask any of Mays' contemporaries about him, and they'll summon memories from his reign with the Giants that remain as clear and sharp as freshly laid chalk in the batter's box.

These recollections are kept alive by talking, so let's allow people to talk, as Joe Torre did on one brilliant Saturday at AT&T Park in June 2007—his final year as Yankees manager. After I lobbed one introductory question about Mays, Torre dove into his subject and didn't come up for air until nearly 10 minutes passed. A couple of New York writers approached me and asked with dry, friendly sarcasm, "Did you get what you need?"

An excerpt from Torre's remarks illustrated Mays' uncommon balance of ease and eagerness. "Willie was a relaxed player," Torre said. "I used to catch behind him. I tried not to call the signs too soon, and he used to yell at me because he wanted to hit right now. One time I asked Willie a question, and as he was answering me, he hit a ball out of the ballpark."

A young Torre sensed immediately that Mays stood apart from everyone else. "Just his body language called attention to him," Torre said. "His rookie year, I guess, was '51. I was 10, 11 years old, and it was fun growing up a Giants fan in New York with a player like that."

"I've answered the question a million times—'Who's the best player you ever saw?' Hands down, it's Willie," said venerable Los Angeles Dodgers broadcaster Vin Scully.

Players who doubled as students of the game knew that they were in a master's presence. Mays' baserunning skills, for instance, were widely heralded. No less a figure than Ty Cobb was quoted as saying that Mays restored the art of base running to the game. Alou, who became a manager after a superb 17-year playing career, was more specific. "He's the best guy that I've ever seen—I haven't seen anybody close—who could score from third base on a short wild pitch or passed ball," Alou said. "This guy would score standing up. What an incredible sense of base running."

Giants broadcaster Lon Simmons recalled watching Mays score from first base on a one-hop line-drive single to left field against Philadelphia.

"He rounded second base, trying to tempt the outfielder to throw it to third," Simmons said. "He threw the ball to second, and Mays just kept on going."

Mays derived special pleasure from this particular facet of his performance.

"Just show me a game where you can create things for yourself, like running the bases," he said.

Or playing center field.

"Mays played center field like a shortstop," Scully said. "In other words, on a base hit to left center, right center, straightaway—Mays had not even the shadow of a doubt that the ball would get away from him. He would field it like a shortstop—on the dead run, coming up throwing. I always marveled at that." Said McCovey, "He did so many remarkable things, it actually became routine. We were so spoiled. He'd make plays that people would yell and talk about for months. We saw those plays every day, so it was no big deal. Hitting four home runs in one game probably was the least of the spectacular things he did."

Ah, yes, Mays' epic eruption. The four-homer game, April 30, 1961, at Milwaukee. This afternoon yielded bushels of Mays folklore. Late the night before, he was rendered suddenly and violently ill by devouring a plate of ribs. "Yes, [ribs] is what it was," McCovey confirmed. "They were famous in Milwaukee then. We were rooming together at the time. There were doubts about whether he was going to play the next day, to be honest with you. He wasn't deathly sick, but I was afraid. I had to wake up our trainer in the middle of the night to get him up to the room. And because I was his roommate, it was going to be my fault."

Come morning at Milwaukee County Stadium, Amalfitano, then a Giants utility man, asked Mays, "What are you from one percent to 100 percent?" Mays replied, "Maybe 70." Amalfitano declared, "Well, your 70 is going to be better than whoever goes out there for their 100."

That convinced Mays to try playing. Again, Amalfitano abetted him. "He had a 35-inch, 33-ounce Adirondack bat that was too light for him," Amalfitano said. "I used it in batting practice because it was heavier than mine and I could try to get my hands going. When I hit it right in BP, the ball would come off that bat much better than it did off of mine. It had two or three knots in the barrel and a nice, wide grain. I said, 'Willie, you oughta try this.'"

Said Giants left-hander Mike McCormick, "Each time he came up, he'd hit one more, you'd wonder when it might stop. We were all in awe." Amalfitano recalled, "After he hit the third one, he said, 'Don't let anyone touch that bat.'"

Alou treasured the memory. "I hit a home run that day and never made the newspapers," he said. "I didn't mind. He would always outshine the team."

But he didn't mean to do that. To Mays, the final score was more important than personal glory. He said, "If I had hit four home runs like I did in Milwaukee and we lost the game, what good are those four home runs?"

For me and many others raised as Mays acolytes, our world spun off its axis when the Giants traded him to the Mets on May 11, 1972. For most of us, big business meant working a newspaper delivery route. We didn't understand that Giants owner Horace Stoneham was hemorrhaging money and had to trade Mays not just to save a few bucks for himself but also to guarantee that Mays would be taken care of financially. Apparently, Lon Simmons didn't fully understand it either. That night, instead of conducting some vapid interview or analyzing a few statistics, the incomparable Simmons devoted his pregame radio show entirely to the trade, since it was the only story worth discussing. Simmons' barely veiled contempt for the deal was obvious on the air; even the transcript of his remarks that follows might reveal his belief that a star of Mays' magnitude must never be traded under any circumstances. Here's what Lon had to say:

Tonight I'd like to talk to you about Willie Mays. As most of you know, Willie was traded to the New York Mets today for right-handed pitcher Charlie Williams and money believed to be a half-million dollars. The theory or philosophy of the trade is for the ballclub to explain. My feelings can only reflect the 15 years I've known the man. Trades are a part of the game, to coin a cliche, and I've regretted the departure of other friends from the ballclub. Willie has seen the same thing and felt the same regret. He was disappointed when Hal Lanier went to the Yankees this year—Lanier, probably Mays' best friend on the club. Even trades of that nature could not have prepared Willie for today, however—a superstar, a fixture, a franchise and not have to worry about a transplant. However, the trade will not dampen Willie's enthusiasm for the game, nor will it mine. Although I must confess a small closet in my mind will be locked, only to be opened when I recall the fantastic things the man did on a baseball field. The sight of Willie scoring from first on a bunt, running out from under his cap in chase of an impossible catch, the number 24 that always meant excitement when it appeared at the dugout steps. This isn't a eulogy for Willie; he's alive and playing in New York. But it is the end of an era. Mays was the Giants; the Giants were Mays. People have tried to fit Willie into notches not meant for him. His excellence in baseball is so great that it's been overlooked by people who criticize him for not having skills he neither professes nor possesses. Willie's job is in the entertainment field, using a glove and a bat and his legs. He is possibly the greatest entertainer ever, as attested by the millions of fans and the fact that he was able to delight two generations of them in a world that changed so drastically in 20 years.

Sentiment is for the ones who can afford it or those who don't have to pay for the luxury. Luckily you and I don't have to pay, so we can be sentimental about Willie Mays.

Simmons proceeded to play a taped interview with Mays which was free of controversy. Unable to contain his sense of humor, Simmons asked Mays whether he'd miss the Blue Chip Stamps that players received for being pre- and postgame show guests that could be exchanged for merchandise. Fans who weren't yet ill or weeping uncontrollably were treated to a collection of Mays highlights narrated by Russ Hodges—his NL record-breaking 512th career home run, his 3,000th hit, and a sequence in which he scored from first base on a bunt by McCovey that went for a double (re-read that one slowly several times and try to picture it happening. Right; I can't imagine it, either). Brief interviews with Giants manager Charlie Fox and a stunned Williams followed. Then an untethered Simmons returned:

Charlie Fox called a clubhouse meeting before tonight's game to tell the players the trade was one that eventually will be for Willie's financial advantage. For some, like Bobby Bonds, who was in tears, it was a near-unbearable loss. For others, maybe the chance to play their way into stardom. But, whatever, the general feeling was sadness on the part of the ballplayers young and younger, because there are very few veterans on this ballclub. So, an era ends. No. 24 will be retired to the Giant trophy room. And the question now, will the Giants be the Phils or the Astros or the Reds? Or will a Bonds or Henderson or Kingman one day make them the Giants again? Can Candlestick Park furnish the background for an act that nearly matches the greatest one in show business that opened in 1951, with Willie Mays in center field?

And that is our Giants warmup for today.

Despite how all this must sound, I really do try to avoid sheer idolatry. The importance of this tapped me on the shoulder before the April 18, 2015, game when the Giants received their championship rings from the previous year's World Series. Mays participated in the on-field ceremony. During the performance of "The Star-Spangled Banner," I watched him shift his weight from foot to foot and bounce on the balls of his feet as if he were a restless athlete. "Look at that!" I exclaimed to myself. "Willie wants to be out there playing."

I soon was disavowed of this silly notion. "He's cold," a Giants official later told me. "He was moving around to try to stay warm."

CHAPTER 3
2010

Edgar Renteria wanted his teammates' attention. He barely had to ask for it.

Approaching the end of his 15th year in the majors, Renteria, then 34, would play in a career-low 72 regular-season games in 2010. Three trips to the disabled list idled him against his wishes. Moreover, a sore right elbow forced him to miss 13 of the Giants' final 14 games. But Renteria was a five-time All-Star and two-time Gold Glove winner who had amassed more than 2,200 hits and, at age 21, recorded the World Series–winning single for the Marlins against Cleveland in Game 7 of the 1997 Fall Classic. Renteria's prestige was unassailable. So was the respect he commanded.

October exploits only partly accounted for Renteria's championship cachet. "That obviously goes into it," said Aaron Rowand, San Francisco's center fielder from 1998 to 2001. "But the kind of person and teammate he was meant even more. That carries a ton of weight with your teammates—how you go about your own business and what kind of person you are. And it doesn't necessarily always have to be about performance. It's about who you are. He was always there for his teammates, no matter what. He was the consummate professional."

In this instance, the date was September 23, and the site was the batting cage at Chicago's Wrigley Field that was tucked underneath the right-field bleachers within the historic ballpark's brick walls. San Francisco trailed the first-place San Diego Padres by a half-game in the National League West standings. But the Giants' sputtering offense threatened their chances of leapfrogging San Diego. They had scored two or fewer runs in nine of their previous 13 games. The night before, Chicago blanked them on six hits 2–0. Rookie catcher Buster Posey saved the Giants on September 21, belting a home run among their five hits in their 1–0 triumph.

Giants manager Bruce Bochy preceded Renteria, urging each player to refrain from assuming the entire offensive burden and trust the hitter behind him in the batting order. Then Bochy and hitting coach Hensley Meulens departed, and Renteria had the floor.

As Rowand said, Renteria was there for his teammates. He was there to motivate them.

Though English was Renteria's second language, he succinctly expressed himself to his fellow position players. He recognized the Giants' potential to advance deep into the postseason. But they were on the brink of squandering that opportunity. Tears moistened Renteria's eyes. He knew the joy of winning it all. He yearned to savor that feeling once more, and the Giants represented his last, best hope.

Within 20 minutes, the Giants absorbed Renteria's address.

"It was the turning point for us," outfielder Cody Ross said. "He basically got up there and said, 'Guys, this is it for me, this is probably going to be my last season and I want to go out a champion.' He got emotional and started tearing up, and I was tearing up, and I look around the room and everybody else was tearing up. It was an incredible, incredible experience."

The right man had delivered the right message.

"Everybody loved Edgar," Rowand said. "Edgar is one of my all-time favorite teammates. He's one of the greatest dudes. Everybody should be lucky enough to have played with a guy like him."

"It's almost like we fed off of that," Ross said. "It pumped us up. It really brought us together. You almost wanted to win it for him."

Pitchers weren't present, but they picked up Renteria's vibe quickly enough. Said left-hander Jeremy Affeldt, "He was an inspirational guy because he was this quiet leader who came out and said, 'This is what's in my soul. This is what I think about and this is what I want to feel before the end is the end.'"

Playing on his fifth major league team, left-hander Javier Lopez understood Renteria's overflowing emotions. "If you truly think that you're a family in your brotherhood, you can be truthful and trustworthy with the guys around you," Lopez said. "You'll know that you're in a good spot. You can be vulnerable, and he was."

The Giants matched a season high that night with 19 hits and routed Chicago 13–0. You know the aftermath. Their offense didn't exactly flourish during the final nine games, but nor did it flounder. San Francisco finished 6–3, captured the division title on the regular season's final afternoon, and surged past Atlanta, Philadelphia, and Texas to win the World Series. It was a cherished triumph for a franchise that last won a Series in 1954 and had not captured one since the team relocated to San Francisco in 1958. It prompted mass euphoria among Giants fans, many of whom wondered whether the team would ever savor baseball's ultimate triumph. It did, paced by precise pitching and propelled by a motley mixture of castoffs and homegrown talent.

And, best of all, Renteria had one more good swing in him.

* * *

Optimism abounded when the Giants reported for spring training in 2010. This hardly made them unique. Virtually every other team in every other season is intoxicated by possibilities in February and March. But the Giants' upbeat outlook appeared legitimate. The previous year, they ended a streak of four consecutive sub-.500 seasons. They needed to improve offensively, lacking any true threats besides third baseman Pablo Sandoval. The switch-hitting, bad-ball-loving third baseman hit .330 with 25 homers and 90 RBIs in his first full Giants season in '09. Yet the Giants had reason to hope. They'd have second baseman Freddy

Edgar Renteria, the Most Valuable Player in the 2010 World Series, crosses the plate after homering in Game 5 of the Fall Classic against the Texas Rangers. Fittingly, he's greeted by Cody Ross, MVP of the National League Championship Series.

Sanchez, acquired at the '09 trade deadline, all season. They added power-hitting first baseman Aubrey Huff and versatile veteran Mark DeRosa.

Most of all, they had right-handers Tim Lincecum and Matt Cain, who might as well have been the personification of the Golden Gate Bridge's north and south towers. Winner of the NL Cy Young Award the previous two years, Lincecum was the best show in baseball with his photogenic delivery and dazzling array of pitches. Subsisting on a starvation diet of support—he received the majors' second-lowest average of runs per game in 2007 and 2008—Cain finally experienced a modicum of luck in '09 and entered the All-Star break with a 10–2 mark. Fittingly, that equaled Lincecum's corresponding record.

Other duos won more games than the 29 that Lincecum and Cain accumulated in '09, namely Chris Carpenter and Adam Wainwright of St. Louis (36), Derek Lowe and Javier Vazquez of Atlanta (30), and Jorge de la Rosa and Ubaldo Jimenez of Colorado (30). None matched the charisma of Lincecum and Cain. In '09, Lincecum was named the NL's starter for the All-Star Game. Cain received the call in 2012. Though this is a distinction based largely on achievement, if baseball folks spoke frankly, they'd admit that the pitcher possessing the most perceived entertainment value often gets the All-Star start.

Given their ages—both would turn 26 during the 2010 season—Lincecum and Cain made the Giants the envy of both leagues. One Saturday morning at AT&T Park I spied them striding out of the club-house together for a between-starts catch. I pointed out this sight to whoever was standing next to me and asked, "What would the other 29 teams give to have *that* on their club?" Given the timing of my base-ball indoctrination, I regarded these guys as a latter-day Marichal and Perry—one creative and thrilling (Lincecum), the other impassive and intimidating (Cain).

Rowand comprehended the totality of Lincecum and Cain, from their skill to their significance. Having entered free agency after the 2007 season and knowing that he wouldn't return to Philadelphia, he signed a five-year, $60 million deal with the Giants, reasoning that their pitching made them ready to win, as thoroughbred racing handicap-pers like to say. Rowand wasn't shy about declaring his faith in San Francisco's staff. "Everybody thought I was crazy when I signed there," he said.

Behind every strong starting rotation is a stubborn bullpen, fea-turing (ideally) a shutdown closer. I figured that Brian Wilson, who amassed 79 saves in 92 chances during 2008–09, garnished by 150 strikeouts in 134⅔ innings, was this guy. But I encountered a relatively humble Wilson when I approached him for a spring training interview in 2010. When I asked whether he considered himself an elite closer, Wilson gave me a little smile and shook his head.

"An elite closer is a closer who's part of a World Series win," Wilson said. "If you get that final out in the final win of the season, then you can consider yourself elite."

Every closer should chant this mantra as he enters the postseason.

As the season elapsed and Wilson's status as a celebrity rivaled his status as a closer, his eccentricities might have seemed excessive. In reality, he was trying to help the ballclub, at least in part.

"He understood who he was on the mound in the sense that he's not going to give hitters too much credit," Affeldt said. "He understood the art of distraction—the unbuttoned jersey, the tight pants, the beard—he's getting all these hitters to sit there and you hear them in interviews and they talk about how his uniform is and he said, 'Perfect. You're so focused on my uniform and my beard, you're not even understanding what I'm trying to do to you. I win.'"

* * *

Barry Zito's success was one of the early season's most welcome developments. Thrust under a microscope once he signed his seven-year, $126 million contract before the 2007 season, Zito struggled under the weight of expectations and finished 31–43 with a 4.56 ERA in his first three years with the Giants. Then he won his first five decisions in 2010. Suddenly the "What's up with Zito?" questions came from a different perspective. Zito insisted that he wasn't carried away by his sudden surge.

"If I was breaking the ties between being defined by bad performance, then I've broken the tie between being defined by good performance," he said. "See, I don't operate like a lot of guys. I'm not going, 'Yes! I'm so confident! I'm 5–0!' I'm approaching the next game like I'm—whatever. It doesn't matter. I just want to enjoy the experience."

Rarely did I receive a chance to show off my background as an English major. But Zito's articulation of his refreshed attitude reminded me of Rudyard Kipling's "If," a poem that's frequently cited in conjunction with athletic performance. I quoted Kipling's most pertinent lines in an off-day piece I wrote on Zito: "If you can meet with triumph and disaster/And treat those two imposters just the same..." I then made a photocopy of the poem and gave it to Zito for his edification. "Thanks, Haft," he said, sounding truly appreciative while maintaining his habit of addressing me by my last name.

* * *

Eliciting a quotation for the ages from Wilson and recruiting Zito for my clubhouse literature class didn't necessarily make me a smarter reporter.

Buster Posey rapped three hits in each of his first two games when the Giants recalled him in late May (after one of these games, the always irreverent first baseman Aubrey Huff loudly referred to Posey as "Jesus Christ." Posey appeared dismayed.). Almost immediately, manager Bruce Bochy and general manager Brian Sabean began remarking publicly about the need to get Posey's bat in the lineup more frequently. This obviously meant trading incumbent catcher Bengie Molina to create a suitable vacancy for Posey. But with Posey playing primarily first base, I was wrong-headedly sucked into the mindset that Bochy simply would rest Molina and Huff more frequently.

I continued to believe this would be the case through the evening of June 30, when Sabean agreed to answer a handful of my questions for a story previewing the July 30 trade deadline. That in itself was nothing unusual. Everything else was odd, which should have aroused my suspicions. First of all, Sabean met with me *after* that night's game. Standard operating procedure calls for such interviews to be conducted pregame or during the early innings. Secondly, Sabean seemed to be in a good mood, though the Dodgers had just completed a three-game sweep, which extended San Francisco's losing streak to five games (it grew to seven before it dissolved). So it was a calm, pleasant Sabean who faced me in equipment manager Mike Murphy's office in the Giants' clubhouse. Sabean repeated the now-familiar line about Posey needing to play more. Whatever follow-up question I asked was ineffectual. The next day, the Giants announced that they had traded Molina to the Texas Rangers for right-hander Chris Ray and a minor leaguer. I remain convinced that if I had the presence of mind to ask Sabean whether a Molina swap was imminent, he at least would have dropped a broad hint. Damn. You have to be mentally nimble.

* * *

It didn't seem to matter anyway. San Francisco lost three of four games at Colorado in its first series after trading Molina. Not only did the Giants observe July 4 by losing the series finale 4–3, but the game also was delayed by rain *and* lasted 15 innings. These factors forced me and Andrew Baggarly, the incisive Giants beat writer for the Bay Area News Group, to miss our flights to Milwaukee, the Giants' next stop. We sat at dinner and agreed that the Giants had no chance of winning the division. They trailed San Diego by a season-high seven-and-a-half games and owned a 41–40 record, having lost eight of their previous nine games.

Naturally, the Giants posted a four-game sweep at Milwaukee and won nine of their next 10 games. They rose from fourth place to second and trimmed San Diego's lead to three-and-a-half games.

The race was on, and three players in particular drove the club in July while compiling cartoonish statistics for the month. Posey constructed a "slash line" of .417 (batting average)-.466 (on-base percentage)-.699 (slugging percentage) for a 1.165 OPS (on-base plus slugging percentage). He complemented that with seven home runs and 24 RBIs on his way to being honored as the NL's Rookie of the Year.

Though it's now easy to take Posey's instant excellence for granted, Affeldt pointed out the foolishness of such thinking. "No one knew that he was going to come up and lead like he did," Affeldt said. "No one knew that he could call a game and he was that athletic and could carry a team like he did."

Huff also thrived in July with a .367/.462/.694 slash line, eight homers, and 23 RBIs. Outfielder Andres Torres, who minted one of my favorite stats ever (eight triples in just 170 plate appearances in 2009), had a .317/.383/.644 slash line, seven home runs, and 20 RBIs.

This trio reflected the renaissance of the Giants' front office. Posey, selected fifth overall in the first round of the 2008 amateur draft, sustained the revival of the organization's intent to develop its own talent. Several years previously, the draft was de-emphasized as the Giants searched annually for experienced, competent hitters to serve as quick fixes that would complement Barry Bonds in the lineup. Torres, a minor league free agent, represented a coup for the scouting staff, who showed that competent players can be found almost anywhere if you look hard enough. Huff, who twice exceeded 30 homers in 10 seasons, was a big league free agent but had no serious suitors except the Giants. Torres and Huff had played for five and four organizations, respectively, contributing to the club's "Band of Misfits" image that captivated fans and the media.

Bochy was named the 38ᵗʰ manager in franchise history on October 27, 2006. But he didn't truly become a Giant until the night of July 20 at Dodger Stadium, where Los Angeles clung to a 5–4 lead entering the ninth inning. Don Mattingly, substituting for ejected Dodgers manager Joe Torre, visited the mound to discuss strategy with closer Jonathan Broxton. Instantly after leaving the mound, Mattingly performed an about-face to add a few remarks to Broxton. Bochy immediately noticed this and alerted the umpiring crew. Under Rule 8.06, which forbids managers or coaches from making U-turns at the mound, Broxton had to leave the game, since Mattingly technically visited the mound twice. Sporting a 7.48 ERA, George Sherrill relieved Broxton and yielded Torres' two-run double. Posey added an RBI single off Travis Schlichting. That sealed San Francisco's 7–5 win and Bochy's status as a hero among Giants fans, who won admirers for embarrassing the Dodgers. It mattered little that umpires actually misinterpreted the rule, according to Major League Baseball. Mattingly should have been ejected for ignoring an umpire's warning (one of them was yelling "No!" at Mattingly) and Broxton should have been allowed to face one more hitter. Too late. The Giants' victory stood.

Paralleling Renteria's critical September meeting with the hitters, Bochy and Sabean herded the starters into the former's office—all except Cain, who was assigned to pitch the next day—after an 11–3 loss to last-place Arizona on August 28 at AT&T Park. This left Zito with an 0–6 record and a 5.51 ERA in a stretch of nine appearances. The other Giants starters fared little better, as their 5–13 record and 5.56 ERA for August indicated. One day earlier, the Diamondbacks manhandled Lincecum while thrashing the Giants 6–0. That concluded a shocking month for the staff ace—0–5 with a 7.82 ERA.

Sabean did most of the talking. In no uncertain terms, he reminded the pitchers that the club's fate rested with them. "We gotta do better.

That's the bottom line," a somber Zito told reporters shortly after the meeting ended.

Six years later, enjoying retirement, married life, and fatherhood in Nashville, Zito still recalled the meeting's urgency. "They weren't afraid to address the weak links on the team at whatever point in time," Zito said, noting that Bochy and Sabean stressed execution of such pitching basics as getting ahead in the count, avoiding two-out walks, and refraining from working the count full after getting ahead 0–2. "They wanted to make sure they got our attention, and they did," Zito said.

Result: From September 5 to 24, the Giants limited opponents to three runs or fewer in 18 consecutive games. No team had sustained a streak that long since the 1917 Chicago White Sox. Relievers and starters matched each other's effectiveness. But it all started with the starters—Madison Bumgarner and Jonathan Sanchez, as well as Cain, Zito, and Lincecum, who reversed his abysmal August with a scintillating September (5–1, 1.94 ERA).

"You could see them turn it on, night after night, and they were trying to compete with each other," Lopez said. "That's when good rotations really get going, when they appreciate what the other guy's done and they try to continue that success."

If it seemed like the Giants led the league in meetings, it's mainly because a large percentage of them worked. On September 4, the day after a 4–2 defeat at Los Angeles, Bochy treated the team to a few scenes of the film *Braveheart*. Prominent among the excerpts was Mel Gibson motivating his soldiers. This prompted the playful and fired-up Giants to yell, "Freedom!" at the slightest provocation. Bochy's objective was to remind the Giants that they were involved in a collective effort, not an individual pursuit.

From this point forward, with the possible exception of Huff donning his red thong underwear for good luck, the most meaningful events unfolded in ballgames, not meetings. Despite performing with a roster lean on postseason experience, the Giants exuded a preternatural sense of certainty as they arrived at AT&T Park for the regular season finale against San Diego. San Francisco began the weekend leading the Padres by three games in the NL West standings. The baseball gods complied by arranging for the Giants and Padres to meet in a season-ending three-game series. But San Francisco failed to get that final, essential, clinching victory in the first two games. Nevertheless, after Saturday's 4–2 loss to San Diego, Bochy and Sabean decreed that players *must not* bring packed suitcases to Sunday's game, though the Giants' immediate future featured multiple possibilities:

- If the Padres completed their sweep of the Giants and the Braves beat the Phillies, San Francisco, San Diego, and Atlanta would share 91–71 records. The Giants and Padres would hold a one-game playoff on Monday for the division title, with the loser of that game heading for a wild card playoff game in Atlanta.
- If Philadelphia beat Atlanta and San Diego beat the Giants again, the Padres would be declared the West champions, based on their lopsided 12–5 edge over San Francisco in the season series. San Francisco would console itself with the wild-card title.
- A Giants victory would force San Diego to travel to Atlanta for a wild card playoff game Monday if the Braves lost. But if they won, the Padres would be eliminated.

Symbolism, anyone? The date was October 3—same as when Bobby Thomson hit his home run (1951), when the Giants scored four runs in the ninth at Los Angeles to win a best-of-three playoff series (1962), when Joe Morgan spoiled the Dodgers' postseason hopes with a three-run homer (1982), and when Los Angeles exacted a measure of revenge by eliminating San Francisco, 103 wins and all, from postseason consideration (1993).

Jonathan Sanchez, who made ill-advised guarantees earlier in the season about beating the Padres, stuck to business this time and worked five shutout innings. Entering the game with a .125 batting average, Sanchez launched a one-out, third-inning triple to ignite a two-run uprising against Mat Latos, the foe Giants fans loved to hate. San Francisco triumphed 3–0, drenching the Giants in euphoria and setting up a Division Series matchup against Atlanta.

Sanchez's surge enabled him to claim a spot in San Francisco's postseason rotation ahead of Zito, who wasn't even included on the postseason roster. Their records for their final six starts were basically the inverse of each other's: Sanchez went 4–1 with a 1.01 ERA, while Zito finished 1–4 with a 4.66 ERA down the stretch. At this point, nobody would have guessed that in two years, Zito would be the toast of the pitching staff.

In the middle of the on-field celebration immediately following the game, Bochy found Sanchez, placed his enormous hands on the pitcher's skinny shoulders, and told him, "I'm proud of you."

Pride yielded to awe in the Division Series opener against Atlanta at AT&T Park, the Giants' first postseason game since 2003. The Giants captured a 1–0 decision, scoring the lone run in a fourth-inning sequence of events that wouldn't have occurred today. Buster Posey singled to lead off against Derek Lowe and stole second base, though television replays clearly showed that he was out. "I guess it's a good thing we don't have instant replay," said Posey, who couldn't suppress his characteristic honesty in the postgame news conference. Ross' two-out ground ball barely eluded Atlanta third baseman Omar Infante and sent home Posey.

The rest was up to Lincecum, who struck out 14 while pitching a two-hit complete game. In retrospect, some observers might wonder how the Giants might have fared in the postseason had Lincecum not delivered such a superlative effort. So many of them, Lincecum included, were appearing in the postseason for the first time. Maybe they needed such a dominant performance to set off for the postseason on a proper course.

In fact, none of the Giants underestimated the impact of Lincecum's gem.

A little more than six years later, Ross recalled that spectacle as if it had just concluded. "That game, for me, was a *statement*," Ross said. "'OK, guys. We're probably the underdogs, but look what our No. 1 starter just did.'"

Affeldt observed that Lincecum controlled the game as if he were playing Nintendo. Affeldt added, "I can tell you that what Timmy did probably allowed us to win that series in a way that it said, 'Hey, man, you're putting these guys in a hole and you're destroying their whole morale as an offense.' Now these guys are feeling, 'Not only do we have to make up a game, but we also have to figure out how to hit again. Because he just messed us up.' For me, that was a game that no one's ever going to forget. I sure know that it helped us continue to feel like we had an ability to win. And it wasn't like a 4–3 or an 8–7 game. It was an absolutely dominating game by Timmy that said, 'We are good enough to win this first round for sure, so let's figure out a way to do it.'"

The Giants did just that, capturing the series 3–1. They forged ahead by winning Game 3 3–2 as embattled Braves second baseman Brooks Conrad committed three fielding errors that generated two unearned runs. Affeldt didn't apologize for the windfall of luck: "That's part of the magic that happens, man."

This brings us to the Cody Ross portion of the program. Strictly speaking, the Giants didn't truly need Ross when they claimed him off waivers from the Marlins on August 21. They already had a glut of outfielders, which was thickened when they obtained Jose Guillen from

Kansas City on August 13. But they partially wanted to block San Diego from acquiring Ross. And they still wanted a good ballplayer. Throughout the major league community, Ross' reputation preceded him.

"He played the game right," said Rowand, who opposed Ross regularly when both performed for NL East teams.

Better still, listen to Ross himself.

"The one thing that I had to do as a player was make it about the team," said Ross, who played for eight different clubs in 12 seasons. "I know everybody says that, but there are a lot of guys who have a ton of talent. And I wasn't fortunate enough to be one of those guys. I had to work really hard to get what I had and be where I was. So I knew that if I wasn't a team guy and I was a 'me' guy, I wouldn't last very long in the big leagues. So from a young age, my dad sort of instilled into me that I had to make it about the team. Put the team first and everything else will work out how you want it to. That was something that I lived by and tried to do my whole career. Obviously there are certain situations where you try to have a little bit more 'me' as opposed to 'team.' But it felt like more 'team' than 'me' my whole career. And I never would change that."

Not all the Giants welcomed Ross so heartily. On July 27, Ross hit a two-run homer off Matt Cain. Ross punctuated the moment by flipping his bat with a little too much elan for Cain's taste. So when Ross made the rounds in the clubhouse to introduce himself, Cain didn't immediately shake the newcomer's extended hand. "Why you gotta flip your bat in the stands?" Cain said, mustering as much feigned contempt as he possibly could.

Ross bonded immediately with Giants fans. "Welcome to San Francisco, Cody!" yelled a tall brunette seated behind the home on-deck circle moments before Ross' first at-bat as a Giant on Aug. 23. He responded with an ear-to-ear grin—which came to be a familiar sight—before striding to the plate and singling up the middle.

Ross appeared in 33 regular season games but wasn't guaranteed substantial postseason activity until Guillen was left off the roster. The initial explanation was a neck injury that Guillen apparently sustained. Then came a report about the real source of trouble: Authorities had intercepted a package of human growth hormone being sent to his home.

Maybe things do happen for a reason. Left fielder Pat Burrell, who joined the club in early June, combined with Huff to provide veteran leadership and powerful offense. In 289 at-bats, Burrell hit 18 home runs, seemingly each one in the clutch, and recorded an .872 OPS. But he hit just .143 in the postseason, so someone had to compensate. That turned out to be Ross, whose October would have left any player envious, except for Babe Ruth or Reggie Jackson. Having driven in the lone run in Game 1 of the Division Series, Ross tied the score in the Game 4 clincher at Atlanta with a sixth-inning homer. Then he entered that dimension that mystifies even the greatest athletes. Facing Roy Halladay, who no-hit Cincinnati in the Phillies' Division Series opener, Ross homered twice in Game 1 of the National League Championship Series in a 4–3 Giants victory. Ross proceeded to hit .350 for the six-game series and was named its Most Valuable Player.

"The one thing I try to explain to everybody, and it's really hard, but the number one thing I can say is I was so focused and so determined to get the job done," Ross said. "And there was no way that whoever was pitching was going to outperform me on any given day. I've never really had that feeling before in baseball. I don't know if it was because it was the playoffs and I really wanted to turn up the volume. I was in a zone, basically. It wasn't a matter of if I was going to hit the ball; it was a matter of how hard I was going to hit it. Obviously you go on some hot streaks during the year, but it was a different feeling than any I've had in my whole life."

I can track the progress of this NLCS by what happened at dinner. The night before Game 3, with the series tied 1–1, I shuffled into a tavern across the street from AT&T Park for a quick meal. At the other end of the bar sat Giants second baseman Freddy Sanchez, eating alone. I waited until he was almost done before sidling over to chat. "I wish we could play *right now*," he said. Right now arrived soon enough, since Game 3 was the series' lone afternoon affair. Artists should have set up their easels in foul territory. The October mix of light and shadow was that beautiful. Cain, who allowed one unearned run in 21⅓ innings spanning three starts in this postseason, blanked the Phillies for seven innings in a 3–0 Giants victory.

On the eve of Game 6 at Philadelphia, I was devouring pasta with three other Bay Area–based scribes when a top Phillies scout happened by. He stopped, we chatted, and inevitably somebody made disparaging remarks about the Giants' chances of winning the series, though they led 3–2. Doubting the success of the teams they cover is a favorite habit among sportswriters. Moreover, the Phillies had compiled the majors' best record that year (97–65) after winning the previous two NL pennants. The scout smiled sadly and shook his head. "No," he said. "Y'all are outplaying us."

I wondered what the scout was thinking after the first few innings of Game 6. With the score tied 2–2, Sanchez walked Placido Polanco to open the third inning before hitting Chase Utley with a pitch. It just so happened that Sanchez also hit Utley with a pitch in a 2009 game. This time, both benches and bullpens emptied, though as usual nobody threw a punch. Sensing that Sanchez's focus was shattered, Bochy removed him and installed Affeldt, who was commanded by bullpen coach Mark Gardner to keep warming up while the nonfight flared and ebbed.

This set in motion San Francisco's chain of relievers who made Bochy look brilliant. Affeldt stranded the base runners before pitching a perfect fourth inning. Intending to neutralize Philadelphia's lineup, which was heavy on left-handed batters, Bochy used two more left-handers, Bumgarner and Lopez, before inserting Lincecum in the eighth. He retired just one batter, but that was enough of a bridge for Wilson. Carlos Ruiz hit a line drive with one out and two Phillies aboard, but the ball was catchable for Huff, who turned it into an inning-ending double play.

The Giants had forged ahead with two outs in their half of the eighth when Juan Uribe, habitually a pull hitter, poked a line drive off Ryan Madson toward right field that simply kept carrying and cleared the barrier. Said Ross, "You know when Juan Uribe hits a ball to right field that something special is going to happen."

Thus Wilson had a 3–2 lead to protect in the ninth. He walked two batters and recorded two outs before confronting slugger Ryan Howard, who was batting .333 (7-for-21) in the series but hadn't driven in a run while striking out 11 times. Number 12 came on a 3-2 cut fastball from Wilson, who was quickly engulfed by teammates bellowing like wild animals as Phillies fans booed half-heartedly.

* * *

By this time, Renteria had reclaimed his role as San Francisco's starting shortstop. Pablo Sandoval's disappointing physical condition rendered him unable to defend third base adequately. That prompted Bochy to move Uribe from shortstop to third and use Renteria. Participating in his 62nd postseason game, Renteria went 1-for-3 and scored twice in the World Series opener against Texas, which the Giants won handily 11–7. Renteria's fifth-inning home run opened the scoring in Game 2 before the Giants took control of the game and the Series with a seven-run eighth inning en route to a 9–0 conquest.

The Series shifted to Arlington, Texas, but the championship drew closer to San Francisco. The Rangers captured Game 3 4–2, but Bumgarner, in the early stage of his ascent toward uncharted postseason heights, yielded three hits in eight innings to pace the Giants to a 4–0 triumph in Game 4. Renteria, by the way, went 3-for-4 with a run scored.

Hours after that game I welcomed a visitor to my hotel room. It was Andrew Baggarly, my fellow beat writer and skeptic. You'll recall that we buried the Giants on July 4, convinced that they lacked a winner's wherewithal. As we sipped an adult beverage, Andy floated a question: "How many people," he said, "do you think have covered the Giants since they've been in San Francisco?"

Performing some quick math—number of newspapers multiplied by average number of beat writers—I tried to come up with an answer. But I concluded that my calculations could only be inaccurate, and I told Andy so. But he wasn't interested in a literal answer. Actually, he didn't care if I answered his question at all. He simply wanted to make an observation.

"You know," he said, "that tomorrow night, we could be among the first writers who have covered the team to write the phrase, 'World Series Champion San Francisco Giants.'"

That mere thought was much more mind-bending than the drink I held in my hand.

In Game 5, Lincecum and Texas ace Cliff Lee took turns ratcheting up the tension. Through six innings, neither team advanced a runner past first base. The Giants broke the spell in the seventh inning when Ross and Uribe singled. Huff executed a surprise sacrifice bunt, but Lee responded by striking out Burrell.

Up came Renteria, who predicted to Andres Torres before the game that he would hit a home run. "I was joking," Renteria said later.

The swing he put on Lee's 2–0 cut fastball was no joke. The ball landed well beyond the left-center-field barrier, providing all of San Francisco's runs in its 3–1 victory. After Lincecum worked eight resolute innings, Wilson needed just 11 pitches to finish a perfect ninth and achieve "elite closer" status.

Awaiting Renteria after he crossed home plate was Rowand, the on-deck hitter and the biggest fan of the eventual World Series Most Valuable Player.

"I'm so glad that it was you," Rowand told him.

The Giants had reached the zenith of their existence. After roaring through the postseason with an 11–4 record, they yearned to keep competing. "After the World Series, we were looking for somebody else's ass to kick," Sabean said. However, nobody from any sport or walk of life showed up at AT&T Park to challenge the Giants, so they finally said goodbye to the season with a much-anticipated parade through downtown San Francisco.

A crowd estimated in excess of one million choked the streets. It seemed as if everybody who had rooted even temporarily at some point in their lives for the Giants showed up. Spectators who squeezed together outside City Hall for the postparade festivities were treated to the sight of Huff reaching inside his jeans and whipping out his now-highly publicized red "rally thong," much to the shock of Willie Mays seated nearby.

Surveying the throng (not the thong), Sabean pondered more than just the playful desire for the Giants to decimate helpless opponents. He turned to Baer and said, "This isn't about winning baseball games. This is about families coming together and people coming together and the community coming together around a team. And that's a beautiful thing."

Baer summarized it all by saying, "We're in the business of making memories."

CHAPTER 4
THE CLEANUP SPOT

Looking Back at Lincecum

Conventional widsom dictated that Barry Bonds was the biggest story in the Giants' 2007 spring training camp. His pursuit of Hank Aaron's all-time home run record was in its final stages. His sometimes haughty behavior toward reporters seemed to increase their curiosity about him, instead of repelling them. My MLB.com supervisors even assigned another writer to cover exclusively Bonds almost full-time. Why not? Bonds was poised to dive into history.

That freed me to write about baseball. And there was no better baseball story on the Giants premises than Tim Lincecum.

The first time I approached Lincecum was one of the last times I approached him alone. That's only a slight exaggeration. By the end of the season, Lincecum was well on his way toward replacing Bonds not only as the Giants' premier performer, but also as the "face of the franchise"— the player most immediately associated with the team. And Lincecum's was a joyous face, contrasting with Bonds' oft-glowering visage.

I found Lincecum on this February morning perched in front of his locker, displaying exemplary posture and sporting a crisp look in his uniform and windbreaker, as if he had consulted the regulations about proper major league dress that are posted in every clubhouse. He sat facing everything and everybody, taking in every detail. No slouching, no loosely tucked-in jersey, no veteran's taking-it-for-granted attitude. As the Giants' No. 1 draft choice (10th overall) the previous year, Lincecum was a primary source of hope for a team striving to revive itself. He obviously was serious about realizing his potential. He also looked like somebody who had transferred to a new high school attending his first day of classes. I introduced myself, he (of course) responded politely, and then I listened to him talk pitching. The 22-year-old right-hander discussed the "torque" he employed to give his pitches velocity and movement. In subsequent chats he explained how he would "pronate" his arm to maximize his effectiveness. This guy was like nobody else.

Lincecum truly separated himself from everybody else when he pitched.

A handful of veteran pitchers—I recall Barry Zito, Tyler Walker, and Brad Hennessey among them—lingered to watch Lincecum throw his first bullpen session of the spring instead of heading for their next round of defensive fundamentals. One of them even pulled up a folding chair. Everybody wanted to see the 5'11", 170-pounder (Lincecum's officially listed dimensions) display his impossibly long stride and refine the pitches that would earn him two National League Cy Young Awards, three league strikeout titles, and four All-Star selections.

Before writing my first feature story about Lincecum, I spoke at length to his father, Chris, who was highly influential in developing his son's form and skill. Chris Lincecum mentioned the names of some of the game's greatest pitchers as he talked about proper throwing mechanics. He also scoffed at the widely held notion that Tim would sustain a serious arm injury—"blow out"—before he could accumulate significant major league service time. Chris Lincecum declared that Tim's intricate delivery was not unorthodox, as so many observers suggested. It might be extraordinary, given all of its moving parts. But Chris maintained that it was a well-coordinated sequence that would prevent Tim from premature injury.

My sometimes-excessive ardor for the past, as well as my resolve to remain at least partly rooted in the present, were evident as I attempted to tell fans about this dynamic individual whom they would surely see in San Francisco before too long:

In a sense, Tim Lincecum is a descendant of some of the game's greatest pitchers, including Bob Gibson, Sandy Koufax, Bob Feller, and Satchel Paige. Lincecum's skill, however, is his alone.

Everybody else closely or remotely involved with the Giants recognized just as instantly that Lincecum could be great, not just good. Moreover, he was charismatic on the field and refreshingly free of pretense off the field. Sometimes he was a little too unbridled. "I think I can dominate in the big leagues like I did at Triple-A," Lincecum told me shortly after the Giants promoted him to the majors in May 2007. He had just posted a 0.29 ERA—that's one earned run in 31 innings—in five starts at Fresno. Sensing that his remark could be interpreted as being overly brash, I declined to use it on the assumption that it would make him the target of vengeful opponents.

I didn't need to protect Lincecum, as it turned out. He blew away virtually everybody. He was, as I repeatedly wrote, the best show in baseball. "He made my game-calling easier and fun because I could call anything at any time and he would throw it," said catcher Bengie Molina, Lincecum's most frequent batterymate. "He showed the world how good he was by shutting people down."

A typical plate appearance against Lincecum went like this: he'd throw a first-pitch strike, overpower the hitter with the next pitch, then throw a changeup that virtually burrowed itself beneath home plate. The pitch looked hittable out of Lincecum's hand, so the batter usually couldn't contend with all that movement and struck out. What a refreshing contrast to a typical pitcher, who starts nibbling at the corners after forging ahead on the count. Lincecum *never* nibbled. He was a lion, not a mouse.

"That's what we're missing these days. Very few pitchers go after a hitter on 0–2 and 1–2 counts," Molina said. "But Timmy went after the guy. He told me, 'If I can get this guy out on three pitches, I'm going to go for it. I don't need to set him up.'"

An illustrative concession to Lincecum's mastery occurred in a 2008 game at San Diego. Lincecum struck out a pair of Padres before

Right-hander Tim Lincecum instantly became a favorite among Giants fans—not just because of his success, but also due to his considerable mound presence and charisma. He won the NL Cy Young Award in 2008 and '09 besides pitching no-hitters in 2013 and '14.

Jim Edmonds was due to hit. Showing clearly that he knew he couldn't hit Lincecum, Edmonds squared around to bunt on the very first pitch. Here was a 16-year major league veteran essentially acknowledging that he was overmatched.

The decline began in 2012. Lincecum finished 10–15 with a frightful 5.18 ERA—the highest among all National League pitchers accumulating enough innings to qualify for the ERA title. Though the Giants left Lincecum off the postseason starting rotation, he contributed five excellent relief appearances in October. In 13 innings, Lincecum struck out 17, walked two, allowed three hits, and yielded one earned run. Fans roared when he sprang from the dugout and bounded for the bullpen to warm up during his three relief stints at AT&T Park. Surely this proved that he still had greatness in him.

But Lincecum's ERA remained well above 4.00 year-by-year, though he no-hit the Padres in 2013 and 2014. At some point during his slide, Lincecum referred to himself as a "thumber"—short for "cunny-thumber," which is slang for a pitcher who relies on throwing curveballs and other soft stuff. Indeed, after regularly throwing 95 mph during his peak, Lincecum now struggled to reach 90 mph with his fastball. But I saw a guy who approached batters with the aggressiveness of a pitcher who still threw with above-average velocity. So I half-scolded him and half-pleaded with him as I insisted, "You're not a 'thumber!' And you never will be!" Lincecum smiled as he listened to my outburst of blind faith. In retrospect, he might have been better off if he had adopted a thumber's mindset. But he wouldn't have pitched those two no-hitters.

Through it all, Lincecum remained immensely popular among teammates. "Every time I saw him, I just wanted to hug him," outfielder Cody Ross said. "Just because I'm like, 'Man, you're so good. You have no idea how good you are.' To this day, I love that kid. I miss him.

He was so free-spirited and didn't care about anything except going out and being the best that he could possibly be."

After a 2010 game, left-hander Dan Runzler looked tortured after allowing one of two base runners that he inherited from Lincecum to score, thus inflating the latter's ERA. Runzler waited until Lincecum finished his postgame interviews, then approached him and whispered what was obviously a heartfelt apology. Lincecum's face broke into his familiar toothy smile as he embraced Runzler and reassured him.

I rarely received straight answers from Pablo Sandoval during the six-plus seasons I covered him. Mostly, he repeated platitudes that he thought people wanted to hear. For example, he'd say, "I'm excited" when an upbeat remark seemed appropriate. But when I asked Sandoval to comment after Lincecum broke a slump with an impressive performance, the third baseman exuded sincerity. "I will never give up on Tim Lincecum," Sandoval said.

For years I entertained the notion that Lincecum and Matt Cain could develop into a latter-day Juan Marichal and Gaylord Perry. Lucky enough to have seen all at their best, I believed that Lincecum and Cain could at least approach the excellence of the pair of Hall of Fame right-handers who rode the wave of dominance in starting pitching during the 1960s. Instead, the Lincecum-Cain era ran its course. As 2016 turned to 2017, Cain did have a chance to claim San Francisco's No. 5 starting spot, if he could fend off competition from two or three rookies. Meanwhile, Lincecum must remake himself as a pitcher. "It's very important for him to realize that he doesn't have that 'power' stuff anymore and he needs to get people out instead of overpowering them," Molina said. Maybe he'll have to become a "thumber" after all. But until he retires from baseball or his arm falls off, I will never give up on Tim Lincecum.

Still the Thrill

He had substance, playing between 150 and 162 games per year from 1987 to '90 as he led the Giants' rise from losers to winners. He had style, unfurling a left-handed swing so beautiful that it belonged on permanent display in the Louvre alongside the *Mona Lisa*. He finished his playing career in 2000 after spending seven years with three teams not named the Giants. When he rejoined the organization as a special assistant in January 2009 and appeared at FanFest a month later, he was received with so much zealous adoration that Giants general manager Brian Sabean, who accompanied him to various events, good-naturedly said, "It's like traveling with Mick Jagger."

Will Clark allowed Giants fans to dream, whether their reveries involved World Series glory or his potential path to Cooperstown. San Francisco boasted a handful of standout performers after the Mays-McCovey-Marichal-Perry quartet faded from prominence. Bobby Bonds, John Montefusco, Jack Clark, and Chili Davis all distinguished themselves as Giants. But Will Clark transcended them with the sheer force of his...well, yes, his will. The Giants hadn't had a star so intent on winning since Mays drove himself to exhaustion, was hospitalized, and missed three games during the 1962 pennant race.

"That was the essence of Will Clark," said right-hander Jeff Brantley, the first baseman's teammate at Mississippi State and with the Giants. "He was that way in college; he was that way in pro ball; he's that way, period. I don't want to brand him as a leader, but he's a guy who keeps you on your toes. I don't know that I've ever seen a guy that came to the ballpark every day with more perseverance and determination to kick your butt. That's a tough thing to do, when you're playing 162 games in his spot. He loved the game, number one, but what he really loved was beating you."

Clark did all he could to accomplish that goal during eight seasons

Will Clark displays his classic hitting form during the 1989 National League Championship Series at Chicago's Wrigley Field. Said former Giants infielder Kevin Frandsen, a fan of Clark's as a youth, "It didn't matter if you were right- or left-handed. You were going to emulate him."

as a Giant (1986–93). He hit 176 home runs, batted .299, and made five All-Star teams, but statistics didn't define him. Constant effort did.

"Everybody knew that I was going to be on the field every day," Clark said. "I was not going to take a day off. The only way I was going to get a day off is if I was hurt. They also knew that, if the game was on the line, I wanted the bat in my hands. Not a lot of people like that situation. I lived for that situation."

The Giants hadn't displayed a whole lot of swagger preceding Clark's ascent to the majors. Then again, it's difficult to swagger when you're stumbling, as the Giants did during the two seasons before Clark arrived in San Francisco. They posted an atrocious .395 winning percentage (128–196) in 1984–85. The Giants possessed some capable performers in the early '80s, including Jack Clark, Chili Davis, Jeffrey Leonard, and Bob Brenly. But Clark, with his glare and flair, brought a bounce to the club's collective step. Future Giants infielder Kevin Frandsen, who grew up in San Jose rooting for the team when Clark was at the height of his powers, was among the legion of fans who embraced Clark and all that came with him.

"He's one of the greatest Giants of all time," Frandsen said. "The guys who the Giants have in the Hall of Fame? Will can match up with them. He was the example we would always use as a batting stance. It didn't matter if you were right- or left-handed. You were going to emulate him.

"The way he played, the passion, the fire. Every pitch mattered to him. The scowl, the first pumps, everything that went on with him made us fall in love with him. And then you meet him and he's exactly that way. Not only do you have a consistent player, you have a consistent person."

Will Clark kept on being Will Clark into his retirement. During his first spring training as a Giants guest instructor, he struggled to hit practice grounders to infielders. Well, of course. He literally couldn't get the line drives out of his swing. After a lifetime of striving for solid contact, how was he supposed to purposely rap two-hoppers to the second baseman?

A Peerless Pair

Clark was the player who led the Giants from the depths. Al Rosen and Roger Craig were the strategists behind this effort.

The mid-1980s through early 1990s was a critical era for the Giants. They fought for survival as a franchise, falling short in four ballot initiatives to gain taxpayer approval for stadium construction as owner Bob Lurie feverishly sought an alternative to playing at Candlestick Park. They fought for superiority in the Bay Area market, because the Oakland A's outperformed them on the field and at the gate. They fought for respectability in the highly competitive National League West, which was won by each of its six teams in a nine-year span (1982–90).

When Rosen and Craig took over as general manager and manager, respectively, in late September 1985, they faced a daunting reclamation project in trying to prop up the Giants, much less win with them. The ballclub was on its way to losing 100 games for the only time in franchise history. Rosen and Craig had no choice but to figuratively grab each player by the neck and growl, "Lead, follow, or get the hell out of the way."

Conducting a team meeting that proved to be as pivotal as it was memorable, Rosen and Craig told players that complaining about Candlestick's inadequacies no longer would be tolerated. A grooming code limiting hair length was instituted. Alcohol was banned on team flights. Participation in batting practice became mandatory.

"I'll never forget their speech," said Giants broadcaster Mike Krukow, then a member of the club's starting rotation. "They basically said, 'We're sick and tired of the moaning and groaning about how bad this place is. Unless you guys have figured it out, you guys are complaining the loudest, but everybody else coming in here just wants to get out of here. And that is the greatest home-field advantage if we use it in that regard.' They went on to say, 'If you bitch and moan, you're going to be out of here. We won't tolerate it. This San Francisco Giants team will never complain about this ballpark again. It's not happening. If you want out, let us know. We'll get you out.' It really was a powerful moment in my career to see how a negative can be turned into a positive."

Finally, caps would be worn properly, with the bill facing forward. This was a direct challenge to outfielder Jeffrey Leonard, who frequently wore his cap backward. Craig recognized that Leonard was a team leader—a ragtag team, to be sure, but still a team—and personally asked him to comply with the headgear edict. All eyes were on Leonard when he emerged from the dugout for batting practice with his cap worn backward—which he spun around as he strode onto the field. Rosen and Craig had a key ally.

"Even though Roger was a firm manager, he was more of a father figure," said right-hander Jeff Brantley. "And I think that would go for whether you were a veteran or a rookie. Roger was always the upbeat nurturer, trying to encourage you and keep you in the right direction, and it didn't really matter if you were Rick Reuschel or if you were Jeff Brantley. The lowest on the totem pole or the most veteran guy in the room. It always seemed like he treated everybody the same, very fair. Always the most upbeat guy, even in the worst of circumstances. That's not always the case in today's management style. Nor has it been in the past."

Brantley added that Rosen's management style differed sharply from Craig's. "Al was a sledgehammer," Brantley said. "And you, as a player, were the nail. You don't really need a sledgehammer to drive a nail home. But that was Al's style. And the reason I say it that way is because I thought it was a phenomenal fit. I thought that there were guys who needed their asses kicked and Al provided the boot. But as soon as that boot was applied, Roger was always there to pick up the pieces, get you back going, and pump you right on up."

From 1986 to '90, the Giants built a 443–377 record, won two West Division titles, and reached the World Series once. Rosen and Craig had succeeded beyond anyone's expectations.

Dusty Baker

A player I had known since the beginning of my beat-writing career in 1991 approached me during batting practice at AT&T Park in 2000 or 2001 and didn't even say hello. He wanted to share something with me that he considered exceedingly important:

"Dusty Baker," he said, "does something every day to make each player feel like an integral part of the team."

Let's see—active rosters are composed of 25 players who arrive at the ballpark about five hours before night games and two-and-a-half to four hours before day games. The manager typically meets with reporters covering the team sometime during that period and tapes his pregame radio show. That leaves relatively little time to schmooze with each guy.

But I quizzed several baseball people on this subject, and they said it's entirely possible for a manager to accomplish this on a frequent basis. However, that would require employing the finely honed people skills that Baker obviously has.

"He goes out of his way to do it. I don't know that it's a planned approach," Brantley said of Baker, whose San Francisco–era franchise record for managerial victories (840), which he accumulated from 1993 to 2002, will be broken by Bruce Bochy (838) in 2017.

Brantley played for Baker during his rookie managerial season with the Giants in 1993. They also worked alongside each other after Brantley became a Reds broadcaster in 2012. So Brantley has observed Baker closely.

"There's a human nature in Dusty, and it's probably a God-given quality, that he can sense when a player has had a rough day at home, when he's had some issues in the family," Brantley said. He suggested that as an African American player advancing through the minor leagues when he did (1967–71), Baker became sensitized to the struggles people endure, both big and small.

"I know that Dusty has faced a tremendous amount of adversity off the field, so I think that he can relate to a lot of players when they have tough times," Brantley said. "He just has that knack of changing the board. He can twist it and put it back in a positive direction."

Unforgettable Mitch

I crossed paths with Kevin Mitchell during 1994, when I began covering the Cincinnati Reds and he was in his second season with the ballclub. He was one of the funniest ballplayers I ever encountered, though a lot of his humor was of the you-had-to-be-there variety. He'd entertain his audiences with tales of cronies back in his hometown of San Diego who went by names like Big Stinky Mike. He pantomimed an imaginary woman sliding out of her dress to the tune of R. Kelly's "Your Body's Callin'." He at once spoofed and saluted a particularly dogged reporter by flattening himself on the floor, chest down, and crawling on his hands and knees as if through a desert while pleading for an interview.

I have no idea whether Mitchell routinely expressed such hilarity during his four-and-a-half years with the Giants (1987–91). I do know that I saw him recapture the productivity he maintained in 1989, when he amassed 47 homers and 125 RBI and won the NL's Most Valuable Player award. For the Reds in '94, Mitchell hit .326 with 30 homers, 77 RBIs, and a career-best 1.110 OPS (on-base plus slugging percentage). That, of course, was the season truncated by the mindless work stoppage, denying us all sorts of high drama: Matt Williams chasing the single-season home-run record, Tony Gwynn striving to hit .400, and the Montreal Expos bidding for a World Series berth. Mitchell belongs in this group. In a 162-game season, his numbers would have been phenomenal.

Unbeknownst to many, Mitchell was a keen observer of the game. Early one evening in '94, he watched a reserve outfielder named Jacob Brumfield drill line drives all over the place in batting practice. Mitchell grinned and said to nobody in particular, "Isn't it funny how some guys have one swing in batting practice and another during games?" Translation: don't get seduced by the BP display. Brumfield actually hit a decent .311 that year, but spent most of it on the bench.

Clark pointed out that Mitchell benefited from astute teammates when he broke into the majors with the Mets in 1984: "He had Gary Carter, Ray Knight, Keith Hernandez—a bunch of veterans that knew what the hell they were doing."

It's Never Over Until...

Bob Brenly's bat flip said it all. It wasn't a show of insouciance meant to insult the opposing pitcher. It didn't convey a sense of triumph, though it accompanied a two-out, ninth-inning home run that punctuated a 7–6 Giants victory. Mainly, the act reflected Brenly's relief that an ultimately rewarding yet all-too-harrowing afternoon at Candlestick Park had ended. Tossing his bat aside symbolized that he could put aside this day, too.

"It was a thank-God-this-game's-over-with kind of flip," Clark said. Brenly, San Francisco's primary catcher, was a late substitution at third base for an ailing Chris Brown in the September 14, 1986, finale of a three-game series against the Atlanta Braves. Brenly didn't feel at all uncomfortable about playing third. Most catchers accumulated some experience at the infield or outfield corners, and he was no exception. He played third extensively as a college senior and during his first five minor league seasons (1976–80). Brenly even finished 1986 with 45 appearances at third base, including 37 starts.

However, the crowd of 8,594 might have wondered whether Brenly, then 32, had ever successfully fielded a ground ball in his life. He committed four errors in the fourth inning to help Atlanta amass four runs and shatter a scoreless tie. Brenly botched grounders hit by Bob Horner, Glenn Hubbard, and Dale Murphy. His wild throw after the Hubbard misplay accounted for two runs. Before Brenly, the last big leaguer charged with four errors in an inning was Cubs shortstop Lennie Merullo, who endured his nightmare on September 13, 1942.

At that point, said Clark, "There's a lot of people who would have cashed it in." Instead, Brenly continued to influence the course of the game, but in an entirely different way. He homered in the fifth inning and contributed a two-run single to a four-run seventh inning that tied the score 6–6.

Said Brenly, "It was the most amazing thing. It was the first time I ever really experienced that phenomenon of being in the zone. Everything slowed down. The pitches looked like they were just floating up to the plate."

Brenly remained in this altered state in the ninth inning, after Atlanta reliever Paul Assenmacher retired Candy Maldonado and Chili Davis. "That last at-bat, you almost could sense it coming," Brenly said. After Assenmacher forged ahead on the count 0–2, the becalmed

Brenly worked the count full. "As the at-bat progressed, I knew what he was going to throw," Brenly said. "As soon as the ball left his hand, I recognized the pitch and it was like a balloon floating up to the plate. On the 3–2 pitch, he threw me another slider and that's what I fully expected him to do."

Brenly crushed it for his 14th homer of the season and his first batter's-box celebration of himself. "That was the only time in my career I ever did a bat flip," Brenly said. "It wasn't because I was showing up Paul. I was so ecstatic that the day ended up the way it did, after the way it started."

Back in the sanctuary of the clubhouse, Brenly allowed himself to blow off steam as he expressed how he really felt about playing third. "I can remember him screaming, 'Don't ever put me there again,'" Clark said with a laugh.

Arduous as the experience was, it earned Brenly undying respect from teammates.

"He kept battling. He kept fighting," outfielder Jeffrey Leonard said. "How he stayed with it, that's the moral of the story. He never gave up. Never."

"We all took something from that game, that's for sure. In a very positive way," second baseman Robby Thompson said.

Dravecky's Triumph

A few years later, the Giants received a more compelling reminder of what the triumph of the human spirit is all about.

Dave Dravecky inspired thousands by overcoming cancer in his throwing arm to resume pitching in the major leagues, albeit briefly. By now, Dravecky's saga is a familiar one to Giants fans, but it bears repeating.

Dave Dravecky warms up before facing the Cincinnati Reds at Candlestick Park on August 10, 1989. This in itself was a triumph for Dravecky, who overcame cancer before making his last, brief, spirited stint in the Giants' starting rotation.

In 1988, Dravecky was told that a desmoid tumor was found in his left arm. He underwent surgery in October of that year, a procedure which removed half of the deltoid muscle in his arm and froze the humerus bone in an attempt to wipe out the cancerous cells. Doctors wanted Dravecky to wait until 1990 to try pitching, but he managed to begin an injury rehabilitation stint in July 1989, which led to his August 10 appearance at Candlestick Park against the Cincinnati Reds. Dravecky allowed only three runs and four hits in eight innings and earned the decision in the Giants' 4–3 victory. To a man, the Giants knew they had just done more than win a ballgame. The usually hyper-competitive Clark cared less about winning or losing than about Dravecky, his friend and teammate.

"From a personal standpoint, it was probably the most emotional game I've played. Ever," Clark said.

Dravecky certainly felt a similar vibe, explaining why Candlestick Park, forever ridiculed and now vanished, shall remain significant for him as the site of this experience. "It's a very special place and near and dear to my heart," he said.

Dravecky started again in Montreal five days later, when his humerus bone snapped as he threw a fifth-inning pitch. The fracture was a clean break midway between his shoulder and elbow. Clark recalled rushing from first base and tried to calm the fallen Dravecky by simply telling him to breathe.

Dravecky broke his arm again about two months later during the on-field celebration following San Francisco's 3–2 victory in Game 5 of the National League Championship Series against the Chicago Cubs. An X-ray revealed a malignant mass, forcing amputation of his left arm.

No compendium of the Giants is complete without Dravecky's presence.

More Than Just a Homer

Giants fans remember Brian Johnson's 12th-inning home run against the Dodgers on September 18, 1997, because it delivered a victory that propelled San Francisco to the NL West title. But its true significance was much more enduring.

In remarks made during a local television special, *Tell It Goodbye: The Story of Giants Baseball at Candlestick Park*, team president Larry

Baer observed that Johnson's walk-off drive hastened the ballclub's climb to respectability.

"I think the Brian Johnson home run was incredibly meaningful," Baer said. "It really clicked us into a new era, an era where each year we're viewed as contenders, an era where we're viewed as a stable franchise."

Johnson was briefly startled when he heard Baer's remark for the first time. However, not only did the former catcher appreciate Baer's statement, but he also furnished his own interpretation, which encompassed baseball's labor relations.

"Not so much that it was that amazing of a home run, but the timing of it was key," Johnson said. "I was on the executive board of the union before the strike of '94 and we kept warning the owners, 'Don't force this strike,' because at some point, the fans are not going to take it. They're going to revolt. They're going to get mad.

"But the stats had always shown that baseball had come back from every other work stoppage with a flourish. It had come back with no dip in excitement or fan appreciation or revenue. So the assumption from the owners, which is why they created the work stoppage and then the cancellation of the World Series, (was that) they banked on the fans loving baseball so much that they would never get mad and turn the other way."

History proved that management was sadly mistaken. "The fans really felt like they were being taken for granted," Johnson said. "And they really were upset, from coast to coast. And angry with baseball—players, union, it didn't matter. It was just anybody [associated] with baseball. They were pissed. And they didn't come back in droves. They weren't blindly loyal to the game. And that shook baseball's foundation. Collectively as an industry, we weren't really sure what to do about it.

"If you fast-forward to '97, the Giants had not won the division since before that strike. It seemed like an even longer amount of time. So, yes,

I would agree that the timing of that home run, unbeknownst to any of us at the time, allowed for the fans to re-engage, the whole Bay Area to engage, with the Giants. Because mostly the East Bay was A's territory. But everybody loves a winner. So the way the A's have been since 1997 and the way the Giants have been since 1997, really has led to this renaissance period of the San Francisco Giants to where they are the big dogs."

For this to happen, Johnson added, it has to be traced to "something special, something important. I think the game that day was big; all of the personalities collected on that 1997 team contributed to the moment; the Dodgers contributed to the moment."

Speaking without a trace of boastfulness, Johnson, an Oakland native who was a product of Skyline High School and Stanford University, wove himself into this narrative:

"A local kid who went to high school in the Bay Area, grammar school in the Bay Area, college in the Bay Area, was known to the people in the Bay Area from just being around, and being a local athlete and a local kid, he provides the home run during that happens-to-be-special moment and that kind of pushes an organization over the hump into a new territory that, in hindsight, so many years later, probably was much bigger than it was at the time."

Call to the Bullpen

Start a friendly argument with this topic: Who's your all-time Giants closer?

Do you rely strictly on statistics to make your selection? Or do you lean on anecdotal evidence? Maybe you turn to somebody not listed here, such as Frank Linzy, Sergio Romo, or the vastly underrated Gary Lavelle, the franchise's all-time leader—including the New York era—in appearances (647).

Here are four candidates to consider. All but one began their careers since closers became an integral part of the game. We provide basic stats, a few factoids, and scouting reports from catchers who collaborated with each pitcher.

Stu Miller

Years with Giants: 1957–62

Career saves/with Giants: 153/47

Summary: Miller finished his active playing career in 1968, one year before the save became an official statistic. He was a spot starter in his first four years with the Giants, partly accounting for his triple-digit innings totals in each of his seasons with the team. Miller was indispensable in 1961, when he finished 14–5 with a 2.66 ERA and a league-high 17 saves. He placed 12th in the NL's Most Valuable Player balloting that year.

The catcher says: "He filled the closer role before the terminology was invented. He had the most unique delivery of any pitcher I ever caught. He had a motion where his neck and left shoulder would come through much faster than his arm. And it would just throw the batter off. The batter wasn't used to seeing anything like that. And then after you throw a few change-ups, you call a fastball, it looked like Walter Johnson was throwing the ball. He'd even fool you throwing in the bullpen. I used to tell teammates I'd bet them a Coke that the first time he faces anybody, he'll strike them out. And I won many, many more than I lost."—Hobie Landrith

Rod Beck

Years with Giants: 1991–97

Career saves/with Giants: 286/199

Summary: Sporting a bushy mustache and pausing in the stretch position with his right arm dangling ominously, Beck *looked* like a closer. He also was a three-time All-Star who finished among the top 25 in MVP balloting three times. Nicknamed "Shooter," Beck converted 41 consecutive save opportunities between mid-August 1993 and early May 1995. He established the club's single-season save mark with 48 in 1993.

The catcher says: "In his prime, he had an average fastball with a little bit of life to it and barely an average slider. But his split-finger fastball was a great pitch. It was probably one of the best pitches in the National League when he was at his best. It came at you just like his fastball, but then it would dive. And so you really couldn't tell between the two, so that's what helped to make his average fastball above-average, and his above-average split impossible to decipher."—Brian Johnson

Robb Nen

Years with Giants: 1998–2002

Career saves/with Giants: 314/206

Summary: Though Nen accumulated 108 saves in five years (1993–97) as a member of the Marlins, including 35 in each of his last two seasons with them, he earned his trio of All-Star selections as a Giant. San Francisco's all-time saves leader remains admired for his insistence on pitching in 2002 despite knowing that he was aggravating a rotator cuff tear, which required three surgeries and ended his career after that season.

The catcher says: "All power, throwing 96, 97 miles per hour. But everything cut. Everything moved from left to right, if you're looking at him as the hitter. Sometimes it would move a little bit, sometimes it would move a lot, but it was always hard. In addition to that, he had a hitch, similar to what we see a lot from the Asian players who come to the United States. They have a little hesitation at the top of their windup before they turn to drive towards the plate. Well, Nen's hitch was just as he hit the ground. So he would skip his front (left) foot across the dirt somehow. It was a mechanism to keep him balanced. And then he would come to the plate. So not only do you have this hard stuff coming at you as a hitter, but you also have this hesitation at the most unusual spot. I would argue that no one in baseball history has ever done what Robb Nen used to do with his front foot."—Johnson

Brian Wilson

Years with Giants: 2006–12

Career saves/with Giants: 172/171

Summary: Another three-time All-Star, Wilson tied Beck's franchise single-season save mark of 48 in 2010. Besides popularizing his "Fear the Beard" persona on the mound, Wilson prompted awe from teammates for his proficiency with crossword puzzles. He underwent his second Tommy John elbow surgery in April 2012 and hasn't pitched since 2014.

The catcher says: "He's fearless. A lot of pitchers are afraid of making that mistake that's going to cost the game. Brian didn't have that. He would go all out and he wanted to say, 'You know what? You're *not* going to score on me.' If he wouldn't have gotten hurt, I would have loved to see how far he would have gone, because he had so many pitches. He had a cutter, slider, and curveball. He had a change-up. And he had a knuckleball that sometimes he would tease me with and I'm like, 'Hey, man, you're not going to throw a knuckleball.' He was so talented when he was on. He was amazing. I love Brian. I know people might see him differently because of his personality, but I love that guy. That's the way a closer should be. Fearless. And confident."—Bengie Molina

Not All Streaks Are Created Equal

I come not to bury Pablo Sandoval, but to praise Willie Mays.
From June 26 to July 4, 2011, Sandoval recorded at least one extra-base hit in nine consecutive games, the longest such streak by a Giants player since Mays also had a nine-gamer from July 28 to August 6, 1963. Curiosity prompted me to examine the streaks game-by-game in an attempt to determine their true significance.

With all due respect to Sandoval, his streak didn't deserve to be mentioned alongside Mays' binge, which featured many more clutch hits. Check it out:

Sandoval, 2011

> 6/26 vs. CLE: 5th-inning leadoff double; no impact on outcome
> 6/28 @ CUBS (1): 3rd-inning RBI double, broke 3–3 tie
> 6/28 @ CUBS (2): 9th-inning leadoff double; no impact
> 6/29 @ CUBS: 1st-inning, 2-out double; no impact
> 6/30 @ CUBS: 13th-inning, 2-out HR breaks 1–1 tie
> (Cubs win with 4 in bottom of 13th)
> 7/1 @ DET: 5th-inning RBI double ends scoreless tie
> 7/2 @ DET: 1st-inning, 2-run HR off Max Scherzer opens scoring
> 7/3 @ DET: 5th-inning double with score tied 1–1, sets up
> 2-run rally
> 7/4 vs. SD: 6th-inning, 2-run HR trims 3–0 deficit

Mays, 1963

> 7/28 vs. PIT: 6th-inning, 2-run HR erases 2–1 deficit
> 7/29 vs. PIT: 5th-inning, 2-out, 3-run HR erases 3–2 deficit
> 7/30 vs. PHI: 2nd-inning double, scores game's first run
> 7/31 vs. PHI: 11th-inning leadoff triple, doesn't score
> (SF loses in 14)

8/2 @ CUBS: 7th-inning leadoff HR with SF leading 5–4

8/3 @ CUBS: 3rd-inning, 2-out HR with SF leading 2–1

8/4 @ CUBS: 8th-inning leadoff double with SF up 1–0 (out trying to steal 3B; hits go-ahead HR in 10th)

8/5 @ HOU: 9th-inning, 2-out HR snaps 4–4 tie (Astros rally in 9th to win)

8/6 @ HOU: 4th-inning leadoff triple, scores to break 1–1 tie

Simply Murph

It's possible to be a member of the family without being a member of the team. That distinction belongs to Mike Murphy, the home clubhouse manager emeritus who set the temperature, literally and figuratively, of the team's inner sanctum.

Through 2016, "Murph" had seen every San Francisco Giants home game, making him more deeply rooted in the franchise's West Coast history than anybody. He served as a Giants batboy in 1958–59, then became the visiting clubhouse attendant with the 1960 move to Candlestick. In 1980, Murph succeeded Eddie Logan, another beloved presence, as supervisor of the Giants' clubhouse.

More than perhaps anyone else, Murph nurtures the collegial feeling among players past and present who lend authenticity to the old-fashioned notion, "Once you're a Giant, you're always a Giant." From relatively unheralded yet faithful individuals such as Hobie Landrith, a catcher with San Francisco from 1959 to '61, to legends such as Mays and McCovey, Giants alumni flock to the clubhouse almost daily not just to banter with current players, but primarily to exchange pleasantries with Murph. Consider an afternoon in mid-February 2011, when spring training had barely begun and position players had not yet reported to camp. No less a figure than Edgar Renteria, the hitting hero of the previous fall's World Series, suddenly burst into the Scottsdale Stadium clubhouse. "Hey, Murph!" Renteria yelled, grinning widely. "Where's my locker?" Nothing about this was startling, except that Renteria had opted to defect to the Cincinnati Reds as a free agent during the offseason and should have been looking for his locker about 25 miles away in Goodyear. Obviously, Renteria needed a dose of familiarity before checking into his new surroundings.

Murph feathers the Giants' nest by treating each player with an almost paternal regard. All-Stars and extra men alike command the same attention from Murph and his industrious assistants. And when Murph tends to a player—whether it's to fill equipment needs or soothe a psyche—he does it with care and, when it's necessary, big-league sophistication.

Ryan Vogelsong received Murph's attention as a Giants rookie in 2000 and as a veteran from 2011 to '15. When Vogelsong returned to AT&T Park in 2016 with the Pittsburgh Pirates, he felt compelled one day to spend 20 minutes talking to Murph and catching up on each other's lives. Vogelsong was drawn to Murph out of sheer respect, gratitude, and affection. "A grandfather figure," was how Vogelsong described him.

Said Vogelsong, "You know what makes Murph the best clubhouse guy ever? I came up on a team in 2000 that had a lot of superstars and a lot of veterans. I had a lot of guys on that team who taught me how to be a major league baseball player and how to be a pro and what you're supposed to do and not supposed to do. But, behind the scenes, I had Murph telling me exactly the same things."

Thus, when the well-meaning likes of Mark Gardner, Bill Mueller, J.T. Snow, and Shawn Estes simply lacked time to minister to Vogelsong because they had to address their own career needs, Murph stepped in. "Like, 'Hey, kiddo, I don't know if you should be doing that.' That's what Murph was for me," Vogelsong said. "He taught me things that the other guys kind of forgot about or missed. As much as the guys taught me how to be a pro, Murph taught me more about how to be a pro. When to be quiet, when to speak up, don't be the last one out of the clubhouse before the game starts. Murph's seen a lot of stuff, man. Murph's seen it all. Even though he's not a manager or a coach, he's pretty close."

This simplified Vogelsong's transition to the majors when the Giants recalled him. "They treated me like I had 10 years in the big leagues when I hadn't been there for two days," Vogelsong said. "A lot of that was because I did things the right way. And the only way I knew how to do things the right way was because I had Murph watching my back. What he did for me when I was 23, I'll never forget it."

Though Mark Sweeney echoed Vogelsong's sentiments about Murph, their perspectives differ. Vogelsong was a rookie drafted and developed by the Giants, a baby born in their hospital. Sweeney didn't meet Murph until the latter days of his playing career, when the Giants became the sixth of seven teams to employ him. Yet few men made as profound an impact upon Sweeney, whose major league tenure spanned 14 seasons (1995–2008), as Murph did. During Sweeney's final big-league spring training camp, he felt convinced that he'd be released before Opening Day. Why would the Giants, who were rebuilding their roster with younger players at the time, need a guy like Sweeney, whose primary value was as a pinch-hitter? But Murph wasn't making roster decisions. In Sweeney, he saw a thoroughly engaging person whose charm, as well as baseball acuity, would help him secure a coveted job as an analyst on San Diego Padres television broadcasts in 2012. "He's easily the best clubhouse guy I've ever been around," Sweeney said. "And why I say that is, he made the 25th guy on the roster—which I was, the 24th, 25th guy—feel like he was just as involved as everybody else. He brought an atmosphere, a closeness, that you can't equal anywhere else. And it was simple. It wasn't anything that was forced for him. It was just the way he was.

"He's a parent, he's a friend, he's a confidant, he's a guy who has the pulse of the whole locker room. I love him for many reasons. Honestly, I could talk about him all day long."

Once you're a Giant, you're always a Giant, which to Murph means that you, too, deserve a slice of the franchise's best. Murph often served as the go-between for players seeking an autograph from the club's regal quintet of Hall of Famers—Mays, McCovey, Marichal, Cepeda, and Perry (listed here in order of the unveiling of their statues outside AT&T Park). During Sweeney's stint with the Giants, he asked Murph for some sort of item signed by all five stars. Sweeney envisioned receiving an autographed ball, which was the easiest way to accommodate all five signatures. Instead, Murph gave Sweeney authentic jersey numbers autographed by the corresponding player. Oh, and Murph also gave Sweeney five jerseys suitable for applying each number upon and framing. "It was kind of a matter-of-fact thing for him," Sweeney said. "I thought of it as it was incredible that he would do it for me. But he would do it for everybody."

If Mays happened to feel hungry during one of his clubhouse stops, Murph would serve him a bowl of soup before he could even ask. If a non-roster spring training invitee hesitated ever so slightly as he wondered what to do with his cleats, he'd hear Murph call, "shoesies!" before materializing from nowhere to whisk away the footwear for scrubbing and shining. If any player needed anything, Murph was there to provide it. In this sense, he helped the Giants win. As Affeldt said, Murph's attitude was, "If you need it, and I don't have it, I'll figure out a way to get it because I need you to keep your focus on the field and do what you're supposed to do for this team."

Said Sweeney, "He was a connection to the history. He was a

connection to everything that made you feel good about the San Francisco Giants. If you bring up Murph's name to anyone who's been in a Giants uniform, it puts a smile on their face. If someone says something bad about Murph, something's wrong. And something's wrong with the guy who's saying that."

Echoes of Russ and Lon

R uss Hodges and Lon Simmons were impossible to imitate but desirable to emulate.

As the Giants' play-by-play broadcasters during the club's first 13 seasons in San Francisco, Hodges and Simmons literally set the tone for the franchise as it settled into the Bay Area. All of those squads were winners and most were contenders, affording Hodges and Simmons ample opportunities to convey the excitement generated by the game's finest performers.

Their respective styles were accented by their home-run calls ("Bye bye baby" for Hodges; "Tell it goodbye" for Simmons). Hodges and Simmons both received the Ford C. Frick Award that put them in the broadcasters' wing of baseball's Hall of Fame, guaranteeing that both of their voices will echo throughout history.

Larry Baer, a native San Franciscan who rooted passionately for the Giants as a youth and became the organization's president and chief executive officer, observed that Hodges and Simmons shaped the way legions of fans felt about the team.

Those fans included Jon Miller, Wayne Hagin, Pat Hughes, and Jerry Howarth, who reveled not only in the players' feats but also the announcers' voices while growing up in northern California. Each ultimately secured major league play-by-play jobs, inspired directly or subtly by Hodges and Simmons. Having outlived Hodges by nearly 44 years, Simmons was able to meet these broadcasters and others who admired him so deeply. As Miller said, "Lon's voice was just synonymous with baseball." Here, in their own words, is what Miller, Hagin, Hughes, and Howarth thought and felt about Russ and Lon.

Jon Miller

Like Hodges and Simmons, Miller is a Frick Award recipient, having received the honor in 2010. Unlike many announcers, who are mostly anonymous outside the home city where they do their broadcasting, Miller has become widely known. Before joining the Giants in 1997, Miller was the voice of the Texas Rangers, Boston Red Sox, and Baltimore Orioles. He also handled play-by-play duties for ESPN's Sunday Night Baseball telecasts for 21 years. Miller grew up in Hayward, a little more than 25 miles southeast of San Francisco. Jon's father, Gerald, frequently listened to Giants radio broadcasts while working on domestic projects. The voices of Hodges and Simmons soon enthralled Jon, who estimated that he became a Giants fan in 1961 at age nine.

The theater of the imagination was Russ and Lon taking you to the ballpark. They really taught me the game and taught me about the Giants—Willie Mays, especially. I was far from unique. The whole area was tuned into the Giants. The Giants were huge. They never televised any games. It was a radio experience, and they made it come alive.

When they were on the road they always would talk about how the different ballparks had different perils for the Giants. Pittsburgh had the real hard infield. They'd bring up the Tony Kubek play in 1960, when the ball came up and hit him in the Adam's apple. There was no artificial turf just yet in baseball, but Pittsburgh was the place where ground balls just shot through. Cincinnati had the terrace in left field where all of a sudden the left fielder going back on a fly ball had to run uphill. They would always give you those descriptions about how each ballpark was so different. That added to the layer of intrigue as they traveled from place to place. That's part of the attraction of baseball. Each park makes the game different, which is something that has not really changed to this day, even though we went through the era of the cookie-cutter, multi-purpose ballparks. Russ and Lon brought that out for me.

I was such a huge fan of the game that even when there was no game on, I wanted some baseball. I had a lot of buddies in my neighborhood; we'd go out and play catch, and if we got a few guys together we could go to the field at the school and play some baseball. If none of that was going on, I'd make up baseball games in the living room. I would make a little field on the living-room carpet. My mom had a metal letter-opener that I used for a bat. I don't remember what I made the little baseballs from, but I would hit them and broadcast the thing to nobody in particular. I was like this nine-year-old nitwit sitting there and making crowd noise. I thought Felipe Alou's name was Felipe Falou. My dad was sitting there reading the newspaper while I'm playing this game and broadcasting it, and he finally said, "Son, it's Felipe Alou." I was like, "Oh."

Around '62 or '63 I sent away for a game called Strat-o-Matic, which was a table-top game. And I would broadcast those games and do the crowd noise and the organist, just to make it more fun. It was an odd thing as you walked in on me. I was in the middle of the roar of the crowd or something. I just thought it was more fun to play those games with it. And I was doing my Russ and Lon impressions, because that was the way I enjoyed the game.

Somewhere in there I guess I thought that it would be really cool to be a broadcaster. In high school I bought a tape recorder, and I was always looking for ways to broadcast the game, maybe off the television when they started televising a little more often and, ultimately, bringing the recorder to the ballpark in high school and when I got to college.

One of my professors at College of San Mateo, Dan Odum, made an appointment with Lon. We went into the booth at Candlestick and I got to talk to Lon a little bit. I gave him a tape of a Giants game I had done. Later on he sent me a nice letter and said he definitely thought I had ability, but I had so much information that he thought I could focus on the hitter a little bit more instead of always, between pitches, trying to get all this information in. He said it was great to be that prepared but not to worry that that was the whole point. I remember always taking that to heart.

I was doing Red Sox games when he started doing A's games with Bill King and they came to Fenway Park. I went down on the field during batting practice to seek them out. I introduced myself to Lon and said, "You did this meeting through my professor and I always appreciated that you took the time to listen to my tape and give me encouragement and tell me I had some real ability." So I'm kind of going on about it and he said, "You know, the more you talk, the more it's coming back to me. That part about when I said I thought you really had ability—I didn't mean it." That was total Lon. We had a good laugh over it.

When I was in Boston and Baltimore and even before that in Texas, when the team I was with hit a home run, I would say, "Tell it goodbye!" I thought it would be fun to have a home-run call. And so I said, the hell with it, I'm just going to go with Lon's call. In those days, there was no XM Radio. The only way you could hear somebody else's broadcasts was if you were in their town or late at night in your car radio if they were on a powerful station. But when you were back East or in the middle of the country, you weren't hearing KNBR or KSFO. And people liked it. Then I came out to do the Giants games and I said, "Well, I can't use 'Tell it goodbye' here. That's already taken." So I just dropped it. But for a while, I co-opted that from Lon. It was like my personal tribute to him.

Ultimately, the main impact of Russ and Lon from a practical standpoint, other than inspiring a fascination and a love of the game in me, was that sort of by osmosis, they taught me how it was done. Years after I started doing play-by-play as a kid on my little tape recorder, my mom found some of these tapes in boxes, and it's kind of embarrassing to hear myself at that age. But actually, I seemed to have an intuitive feel for how to do it, to paint a picture of a play while it was in progress. It wasn't as if anybody taught me or I took a class in it. I just seemed to have that knowledge and those were the guys who taught me without my knowing that they were doing it.

Wayne Hagin

Wayne Hagin was a play-by-play announcer for six major league teams spanning 1981 to 2011. He grew up in San Jose and graduated from Blackford High School in 1974. By then, he had been bitten by the broadcasting bug, which was spread not only by Hodges and Simmons but also Bill King, the dramatic voice of the Raiders and Golden State Warriors at that time. "I was 14 years old when I knew I wanted to be a broadcaster," Hagin said. It was Hagin's good fortune to begin his big league career behind the microphone with the A's from 1981 to '84, just as Simmons launched his 1981–95 stint with Oakland and joined Bill King in the broadcast booth. Said Hagin, "People often ask me what it was like to grow up in the Bay Area and to eventually work side by side with Lon Simmons and Bill King—to learn broadcast and life lessons from two icons. I answer simply, it was one of the true blessings in life." Shortly after Simmons died at age 91 in April, 2015, the Giants hosted a private ceremony at AT&T Park to celebrate his life. Hagin, who also was a Giants broadcaster from 1987 to '88, was among the speakers at that event. Here, he recalls the singular experiences he shared with Simmons, including a visit to the retired broadcaster's home in Maui in 2012.

Lon became a friend. That was the true blessing for me. How in the world do you become friends with somebody who you idolize?

I went and saw him in Hawaii in 2012. I knew he was suffering and that probably was my last chance to see him. I flew in there from Denver for three days. And it was the greatest three days of my life. I had the opportunity to just sit and listen.

To give anybody an idea of what Lon was really all about, he picked me up at around 9:15 at night. We started going down the straightaway from the airport and I said something to him. He always knew how I felt about him as a broadcaster. And he pulled over to the side of the road very quickly, abruptly. He put the car in park, looked at me, and said, "Now, I'm your friend. And I consider you my friend. We don't have that much time. Let's not talk about broadcasting. I know you respect me. That's okay. But we're friends. So while we're here, let's talk about friendship."

We would sit in his living room—he'd be on the couch and I would be in the chair—and he'd fall asleep. I'd be thinking, Aw, shucks. It's 7:00 at night. I thought, What a wasted opportunity. I won't get to talk to him today. Well, lo and behold, in five minutes, he'd wake up, and we'd talk until midnight. And he was nonstop.

Over the years of our friendship, I had not heard much about his dad, so he reflected on him a lot. He reflected on his marriages, because I knew his second wife, not his first. And he talked about Willie Mays a lot. He told me that Willie would say, "I'm in a slump. Can you and Russ figure out what I'm doing wrong at the plate?" Because this was before the advent of television and video. So the relationship they had was so special.

There were two stories he told me in Hawaii. Years earlier, he purchased a home for his mother in Palm Springs, because that's the kind of guy he was. He went out with Ken Venturi, the golfer. Well, Ken Venturi was dear friends with Frank Sinatra. And so Lon met Sinatra. He was invited to this party to go out to dinner with Sinatra at a club. He took a female friend who he knew in Palm Springs with him. And he got up from the table with his friend to go up to dance. And Sinatra's bodyguard went over to the dance floor, tapped Lon on the shoulder, and said, "You're not supposed to be dancing." Lon asked, "Why?" "Because Frank doesn't dance. You're at his table. You need to stay at the table."

It's Christmas morning, 1973, in Palm Springs, and he answers the phone. The caller said, "Hey, Lon, it's Frank." Lon said, "Frank who?" It was Sinatra. Frank felt for him; he knew that Lon's first wife had just died. Frank said, "I want you to come over and have Christmas with us." And here's Lon going, "What?" Frank said, "Yeah, and who's there? Your mother, right? And Lon said, "Yes, but I also have my two daughters." Frank said, "Bring them!" So within an hour, they're at the Sinatra compound in Palm Springs. They walk in and there are presents for all three of the women and Lon. That's the effect that Lon had. It says a lot about Sinatra. But it also said a lot about Lon. The Bay Area would never know that Lon was invited to Frank Sinatra's house for Christmas. This icon was reaching out to Lon because he had lost his wife.

He was the most unbelievable guy ever. The most giving. In 1982, we flew to Baltimore. Jay Alves, the A's team statistician who later became media relations director, and I must have been wondering aloud how far we'd be from the White House, because we had never been to D.C. Lon overheard us. So we land in Baltimore in the early evening, and we each get a phone call from Lon telling us to be in the hotel lobby at 9:00 the next morning. Lon got a limo and took us to the White House and the surrounding area. He did that stuff all the time.

And you knew that he took the entire A's team to his country club for dinner in Palm Springs—twice—when they played the Angels during Spring Training? Canseco. McGuire. Rickey Henderson. Tony LaRussa. The entire team, on his dime. Who does that? And he did not make a mint doing the Giants and 49ers and being the sports director at KSFO. That's the kind of guy he was. Just as generous as you could possibly be. And he learned that from Russ.

I think the movie Pay It Forward came out in 2000, with Kevin Spacey and Helen Hunt. It really struck a nerve with a lot of people. "Pay it forward"—gosh, what a nice concept. That's the way we should live our lives. If I'm not mistaken, July 19 is Lon's birthday. And July 19, 1960, was the day Juan Marichal broke into the major leagues, and he had a no-hitter going into the eighth inning. Lon was doing the play-by-play and was going to hand it over to Russ, who would finish up the eighth and ninth innings. He's the lead broadcaster. He's the veteran. And Russ said, "Keep going." And Lon looked at him and said— this is from Lon's own words—"What do you mean, keep going?" Russ said, "I've had plenty of opportunities to call no-hitters. I've had my fair share. Keep going. You call this." Of course, Clay Dalrymple broke it up with a two-out single in the eighth inning. But Marichal finished with a one-hit shutout in his debut, on Lon's birthday. And Lon could never get over the fact that Russ would do that for him.

So, Lon became the premier broadcaster of the Giants, then went over to the A's. The year was 1982. The A's were at Milwaukee County Stadium. Lon was at the microphone on radio, Bill King was on television, and a way-too-young Wayne Hagin was sitting next to Lon. It was the third inning, and Rickey got aboard. He had 118 stolen bases, so he was tied with Lou Brock. If he swipes second base, he becomes the all-time single-season stolen-base king. And Lon relived the moment that Russ had lived for him. He said, "Wayne, put on your headset. You're going to call this. This call's going to be in the Hall of Fame." Lon Simmons tried to give that call to me, all based on paying it forward, from Russ Hodges in 1960. This is 22 years later, and he's trying to do the same thing for me. I got up, walked to the back of the booth, and said very loudly, "Only one guy deserves to make this call, and he has the headset on." Sure enough, the next pitch, Rickey took off. And listen to that call. It's a great call by Lon, with Rickey stealing second base. But think about it. Vin Scully, Jack Buck, Ernie Harwell, Harry Caray—no knock on any of them. But who was going to give up that call? Not a single one of them would have given it up. But there's Lon Simmons trying to help me, a guy in his second year in the major leagues, overshadowed completely by Lon and Bill. They knew I had a great opportunity at a very early age. Lon always said that. I got the job when I was 24. He was 36 when he got his first major league job. So he always told me, "You got a head start on me. Let's sharpen the skills. Watch, observe, and listen." But nobody ever knew why he did that in 1982. And why he tried to do it again when Dave Kingman had hit three home runs in a 1984 game at the Kingdome in Seattle. Once again, he wanted to give the microphone to somebody else. It wasn't until I went and saw him in Hawaii that I found out why he did that.

He and Russ loved each other. They were friends on the air. They were friends off the air. That's the difference between today and their day. In my opinion, that's why we were drawn to Russ and to Lon. They were like family. That's hard to find in broadcast booths today. Everybody competes. It's too bad. Are those guys family, or are they workers together? That's why I think the Russ Hodges–Lon Simmons relationship was so special, as I got to know it down the road by getting to know Lon and hearing about Russ and the different things they did together. That's why Willie Mays, Willie McCovey, and Jimmy

Davenport were at Lon's memorial service. They felt as if a member of their family had passed away.

When John Wayne died, someone said, "America has lost its last hero." But the person who wrote or said that never met Lon Simmons.

Pat Hughes

Pat Hughes appreciates what he does, where he has been, and who came before him. That became apparent in recent years when he put together Baseball Voices, a series of CDs that honored and highlighted the work of Mel Allen, Red Barber, Harry Caray, and other broadcasting legends—including Hodges and Simmons. The Chicago Cubs' play-by-play announcer since 1996, Hughes also assembled a CD featuring memorable moments from the Cubs' World Series–winning 2016 season that ended the franchise's 108-year streak without winning a title. Hughes grew up in San Jose and graduated from Branham High School and San Jose State University.

You really start to love baseball when you're eight, 10, 12 years old, and you automatically think your announcers are the greatest in the world. Of course, you have nobody to compare them to. You just know that you love them and that they really are heroes. I loved playing sports, reading about them, watching games on television, listening on radio every day, and we had Russ and Lon. The amazing thing is that my feeling now as a 61-year-old is almost exactly the same. Russ and Lon were two of the greatest ever. Both were Hall of Famers, both knew the game, had great voices, were very smart, were very dramatic, had distinctive home-run calls, and loved the Giants. You could tell they got along with each other, so they just kind of naturally made you become a Giants fan, every bit as much as Willie Mays; Willie McCovey; my favorite, Orlando Cepeda; Juan Marichal; Gaylord Perry; and you can name anybody else that played for the Giants at that time. And if you think of Russ and Lon as a partnership, you'd be hard-pressed to find any other duo on radio in baseball history that was any better than Russ and Lon. Really hard-pressed.

What a lot of people don't realize is how smart both men were. Russ Hodges had a law degree from the University of Kentucky, if I'm not mistaken. But he needed to make some money and never really did practice law. Lon was also extremely bright. If you listen to his writing for the pregame show on the day Willie Mays was traded, it's tremendous. It really is. Lon was very well-read and I think that's one of the things that was kind of overlooked regarding Russ and Lon—just how bright, aware, and sharp both men really were.

They loved the Giants. You could tell they were both huge Giants fans. And a fan senses that. A fan picks up immediately how a broadcaster feels about the team. If they love the team, they want the announcer to love the team. There's no two ways about that. If you're going to be a longtime voice covering a baseball team, either you have to love that team or you have to be a great actor and make it sound like you love that team. Because the fans want you, need you, to love that team as much as they do. And there was no question that Russ and Lon loved the Giants.

I kind of sensed from Lon that he was a little more rebellious than Russ was. Lon had some discussions with management, and they wanted him to be a little bit more of a homer. He said, "I can't do that. I have to give you the game right down the middle." And I think in the Bay Area, that was appreciated. I don't think the Bay Area really wants you to be a homer. There's a difference between loving a team and being a homer for that team. It's a fine line, but I think it does exist. There's a difference.

And I'll tell you one thing: Lon Simmons' voice has to be one of the top 10 voices ever among American performers. Not just baseball announcers, but singers, newsmen, reporters, broadcasters, you name it.

CHAPTER 4: The Cleanup Spot

Lon Simmons' voice is way up there among the all-time greats. We used to have this little stereo in my hometown of San Jose—a little hi-fi, we used to call it—and it had these big speakers on either side. I used to love to get down near the speakers and listen to games. And to hear Lon's voice, it was almost from another world. It was almost not human, it was so great. And I'd say Jon Miller is almost in that same category.

I wanted to be a player when I was a kid. I wanted to play NBA basketball or big league baseball. I was a decent amateur athlete—I was all-conference in high school—and then I played one year of basketball in college at San Jose State and I realized I wasn't good enough. So I thought about being a broadcaster immediately once I realized I was not going to be a player. We had some tremendous role models for any aspiring broadcaster in the Bay Area. We had Russ, we had Lon, we had Bill King, we had Al Michaels for a while. At night I could tune in to Vin Scully. I think the whole package of all of those guys probably had a lot to do with me going into it. I have to be honest and say that it was my love of sports and wanting to be a player first and then the next best thing would be to become a broadcaster. But I'm sure that Russ and Lon had something to do with it. I'm not sure I can quantify exactly what percentage. They certainly were a factor.

Jerry Howarth

Jerry Howarth's road to becoming the Toronto Blue Jays' lead play-by-play announcer began in Santa Rosa, California. Intent on shortening his commute to San Francisco, Howarth's father moved the family to Novato. Howarth graduated from Novato High School in 1964 and from Santa Clara University in 1968. Before that, he was among the thousands of Bay Area youths whose ardor for baseball was fueled by Hodges and Simmons. "They were such a huge part of my growing up," said Howarth, who has been behind the microphone for the Blue Jays since 1981.

In 1957, my dad took me to a baseball game at Seals Stadium to see the San Francisco Seals play the Hollywood Stars. That was Triple-A, of course. I thought, this is pretty good, and I played Little League baseball myself when I was growing up. And my team was the Giants! That was kind of cool.

But in 1958, when the Giants came out, all of a sudden that changed dramatically. For me, not only was it Willie Mays and Orlando Cepeda and the next year Willie McCovey, but it was also games on the radio, and that was Russ Hodges and Lon Simmons. The only games we saw on television were the three series played down in L.A., where we saw nine Dodgers games, and that was it. So everything was radio.

I was eight years old when I went to my first 49ers game; my parents were season-ticket holders at Kezar Stadium. They sat on the 35-yard line, about 25 rows up, and the only games I got to see were at the end of the year. The Green Bay Packers would come in— they'd won two games, and they had this young coach named Vince Lombardi but they were awful. They were 2–10 all the time, so my mom said, "I'm not going to watch those Packers play," and I said, "I'll go." And so I got to watch the beginnings of Vince Lombardi and Bart Starr. The next week, this next team would come in and they were, like, 2–10 as well—they were awful—and that was Don Shula starting his career with the Baltimore Colts and a young quarterback named Johnny Unitas. I got to see those two games at Kezar Stadium for about two or three years because my mom didn't want to go. And I'm suddenly getting more and more into sports. But Lon Simmons was calling the games on the radio. And here I am, a devout 49ers fan then and now, win or lose, all of a sudden Lon Simmons made the 49ers come alive for me. It was so important for me as a broadcaster, because he painted a picture. I loved his enthusiasm. He didn't shout. He didn't yell. All these things later meant something to me as my own broadcasting career developed, but not then. It was kind of like seeds being planted.

This was another thing that I remember about Russ and Lon on the radio: they didn't come in a lot on each others' innings. They were pretty much two professional play-by-play men and there was no analyst at that time. What I remember as a kid listening would be Russ doing the play-by-play, and there'd be a pause, and Lon would say one thing. It would be short, simple, sweet, and I would burst out laughing. And so would Russ Hodges. I began to appreciate Lon's sense of humor. The game was important, there were a lot of games to broadcast, and while he took his job seriously, in the game itself he found some humor and some ways for all of us to lighten up, enjoy, and laugh out loud, and that's what Lon provided in addition to everything else.

I loved it when Russ was laughing on the air and Lon would laugh as well. But they did it in a professional way. You learn from that, too—that it was the game that came first, not them. They weren't the center of attention. But by highlighting the game and highlighting each other in the booth, they highlighted themselves.

THE FIVE HALL OF FAMERS SPEAK

"They're not just statues."—Brian Sabean

What's special about being a Giant?

Orlando Cepeda, 1B, 1958–66
"Everything. The Giants were the first team to have Latin players. When I was a kid, Ruben Gomez and Valmy Thomas played for the Giants, so I wanted to sign with them."

Gaylord Perry, RHP, 1962–71

"They were like family. The Stonehams knew my kids; my kids knew the Stonehams. We were a close-knit ballclub from the minor leagues to the big leagues. We traveled together, ate together, played baseball together, and played cards together. If somebody knocked my teammates down, I couldn't wait to get him. I spent 10 years with the Giants and played 11 years after that, but I didn't find any bunch of guys who could match them."

Juan Marichal, RHP, 1960–73

"To play with those men—Mays, McCovey, Cepeda, Felipe Alou, Gaylord Perry, Tom Haller, Jim Ray Hart, Jim Davenport, Chris Speier, Tito Fuentes, Garry Maddox, Gary Matthews, Bobby Bonds—I was thrilled to be on that field with all of them. It was a great honor for me."

Willie McCovey, 1B, 1959–73, 1977–80

"The Giants, with the exception of maybe a couple of years, have always run the organization like a family. Horace Stoneham loved his players. And he treated it like a family. I signed when I was 17 years old. I was just a kid. So I grew up in this organization. And Horace took a liking to me. I signed during the time when players didn't bounce from team to team every year or every other year. We stayed together for 13, 14, 15 years. So that made a big difference."

Willie Mays, CF, 1951–52, 1954–72

"I think we have more guys in the Hall of Fame than anybody. That's special, I think. I was proud to just be a Giant because they were the team that signed me and got me out of the so-called sticks of my hometown [Fairfield, Ala.]. I'm just proud to be involved with so many guys that came through the system that I taught. We had good outfielders I taught with what was called on-the-job training."

CHAPTER 5
BARRY

A round noon on April 22, 2016, Barry Bonds headed for home, as he did thousands of times during his 22-year major league career. This trip didn't involve advancing 90 feet at a time, however. On this occasion, Bonds rounded the bases anchored in his memory and scored with his sincerity as he talked at AT&T Park about his Northern California roots.

The occasion was a celebration of the life of Jimmy Davenport, who died nearly two months earlier. Bonds, the Miami Marlins' first-year hitting coach, wasn't originally scheduled to speak. But Giants management wisely scheduled this event to coincide with the Marlins' lone 2016 visit to San Francisco. The lineup assembled to laud Davenport included fellow baseball veteran Joe Amalfitano, virtually the club's entire broadcast team, general manager Bobby Evans, and son Gary Davenport. The affair's intimacy—only a couple of hundred guests were in attendance—encouraged speakers to express themselves freely. And it was Bonds who displayed the most emotional range.

For a few minutes, Bonds was no longer baseball's all-time home run leader. He wasn't the pariah who played his last several seasons under the cloud of suspected performance-enhancing-drug use. He was, however, charming, funny, and sensitive—traits that he rarely, if ever, openly displayed, at least when reporters were present—as he dwelled on the kinship between the Bonds and Davenport families, who lived near each other in San Carlos, California.

Asked about Bonds' expressiveness, Gary Davenport said, "See, that's a side that we all knew growing up. For him to step up and do that publicly, it was a special Barry moment for us."

Jim Davenport and Bonds' father, Bobby, were not only Giants teammates but also inseparable off the field. With his voice breaking ever so slightly, Bonds gripped the audience's attention when he began his talk by saying, "I'm going to tell you a story about a friend—the best friend of my father I've ever seen."

At that point, Bonds asked for his mother, Pat, and Jim Davenport's widow, Betty, to join him at the lectern. Bonds paid tribute to his mother, who raised three sons, and Betty Davenport, who reared five children while their husbands were living the itinerant baseball lifestyle.

"To bring Mom and Pat up with him, that showed a lot of class on Barry's part," Gary Davenport said.

Bonds knew his audience, and vice versa. Among those attending the memorial for the popular Davenport were Giants president Larry Baer, vice president of baseball operations Brian Sabean and other members of the team's front office, as well as manager Bruce Bochy. Hall of Famers Willie Mays and Orlando Cepeda were present. So were Giants alumni such as Amalfitano, Jim Barr, Felipe Alou, Hobie Landrith, Bill Laskey, J.T. Snow, Vida Blue, Terry Whitfield, Fred Breining, Rich Robertson, Rich Murray, and Mark Gardner.

Nearly everybody listening to Bonds knew how baseball's time-consuming, monomaniacal lifestyle can strengthen or sink a family or friendship. Barry told a story of two clans and two men that nothing, not even baseball, could tear asunder.

"I never saw two guys that were like two little boys all the time," Barry Bonds said of his father and Davenport. "Every Monday, Half Moon Bay golf. After Wednesday, Half Moon Bay golf. Friday, they'd go fishing."

Bonds paused and jokingly added that if his father or Davenport happened to be squabbling with their wives, "[they'd] go fishing again."

That prompted laughter, as Bonds did again a few hours later when he addressed reporters before Miami's batting practice. "I haven't had this much good press in my entire life, and I'm liking it. I should've done this a long time ago," he said. Asked whether being nice was what he should have done, Bonds said, "I'm the same. You guys have been nicer. I appreciate that."

Can a man remake his image? Barry Bonds just might be on the verge of beginning to do that—and without a gargantuan effort, as he indicated.

For instance, the stars and planets seem to be aligning for Bonds to gain election to baseball's Hall of Fame. If he remains cordial to reporters, many of whom receive Hall of Fame ballots annually, that can only benefit him. And though the court of public opinion long ago found him guilty of using performance-enhancing substances, he's legally clean. Perjury charges against him for allegedly lying to a grand jury during the federal government's investigation of BALCO (Bay Area Laboratory Co-operative) were dropped. An obstruction-of-justice conviction has long been overturned. Having garnered 44.3 percent of the vote from writers participating in last year's Hall of Fame balloting—up from 36.8 in 2015—Bonds should continue to climb toward the 75 percent figure required for election during his next six years on the ballot.

Judged strictly by achievements, Bonds should have gained first-ballot induction when he initially became eligible in the 2012–13 off-season. If 762 home runs and seven MVP awards don't impress voters, nothing will. Said infielder Rich Aurilia, "I don't think there was a player who played against him that wouldn't say he was at least one of the top two players he ever faced."

A National League scout told me that Bonds knew exactly what kind of swing to put on a baseball to drive it out of the park. That sounded self-evident on the surface. But the remark became easier to appreciate when it was recalled that pitchers frequently skirted Bonds, who hit a single-season record 73 home runs in 2001.

"I couldn't comprehend it. He was getting one pitch to hit a game, and he wouldn't miss it," first baseman Will Clark said. "To have that kind of focus, that is unbelievable."

Bonds maintained that swing and that focus almost constantly.

This was evident as I watched a May 1997 Giants–Reds game from a seat between home plate and first base at Cincinnati. The score was tied 2–2 with one out in the top of the 10th inning. Reds left-hander Mike Remlinger fell behind on the count to Bonds 2–0. At this stage, pitchers would typically avoid the possibility of a Bondsian belt by intentionally walking him. Instead, Remlinger fired a fastball for a strike past Bonds, who kept his bat on his shoulder. Bonds briefly stepped out of the batter's box with his right foot, continuing to stare at Remlinger. It could have been my imagination, but I thought a quizzical expression crossed Bonds' face. His expression said, *Are you challenging me?* Sure enough, Remlinger threw another fastball for a strike. He turned and watched the ball disappear over the left-center field wall.

Tagging along with his father to Candlestick Park gave Bonds a head start in absorbing how big leaguers think and act, succeed and fail. You might say that Barry Bonds descended directly from baseball royalty. Willie Mays was Bobby Bonds' most eminent tutor when the 22-year-old outfielder broke into the majors in 1968. Not so coincidentally, Bobby clobbered a grand slam off Los Angeles' John Purdin in his June 25 debut. Mays was ultimately named Barry's godfather.

Bobby Bonds tried to accomplish the impossible: emulating Mays. For one thing, Bonds struck out too much. He set a major league record by going down on strikes 187 times in 1969, then broke that mark with 189 in 1970. However, Bobby Bonds' merits as a ballplayer stood up on their own. A high school All-American selection in track and field, he possessed Mays' remarkable combination of power and speed. Bobby Bonds was the first player—Barry was the second—to reach or exceed 30 home runs and 30 stolen bases in a season five times.

"I think Bobby could have been among the top three players the Giants ever had," said Ken Henderson, another member of the Giants' staggering stable of talented outfielders that they drafted or signed from the late 1950s through the early '80s. Here's a partial list, besides Henderson, Mays, and Bonds: the Alou brothers, Willie Kirkland, Leon Wagner, George Foster, Garry Maddox, Gary Matthews, Manny Mota, Jose Cardenal, Bernie Williams, Ollie Brown, Nate Oliver, Frank Johnson, Dave Kingman (unless you consider him a first or third baseman), Jack Clark, and Chili Davis.

Bobby Bonds separated himself from everyone else in the realm of clutch hitting in 1973. Using a certain standard for Win Probability Added, a modern metric that measures the change in probability of winning a game caused by each batter during the game, ESPN's David Schoenfield figured out that Bonds won nine games that season with late- or extra-inning hits that virtually reversed the probable outcome (a Giants defeat). The most enduring of those hits occurred in an 8–7 victory over Pittsburgh on May 1, when the Giants scored seven runs with two outs in the ninth inning. Bonds' bases-loaded, three-run double won it. "What a comeback this one was. And what a story this will be," broadcaster Lon Simmons crowed on the air.

You could say that Mays bestowed his baseball acumen upon Bobby Bonds, who then bequeathed it to Barry. After Bobby died of complications from lung cancer and a brain tumor in 2003, Mays provided guidance to Barry when necessary. I witnessed a spring training hitting lesson in 2005, my first year on the Giants beat. Mays sat in a folding chair outside the batting cage but as close to the right-handed-batter's box as possible, giving himself a full view of Barry Bonds in the left-handed side. After approximately 20 swings, Bonds suddenly lost all semblance of his timing. He could barely hit the ball out of the cage, and when he did, he generated ineffectual fly balls and grounders. Members of the media weren't allowed near the cage, but we could see Mays saying something to Bonds, who resumed

In his guise as the Miami Marlins' hitting coach during the 2016 season, Barry Bonds acknowledges cheers from the fans who always will be his at San Francisco's AT&T Park.

swinging—and hitting. Line drive. Another line drive. A cluster of home runs. During their collaboration, Mays probably uttered nothing more than a few dozen words to Bonds. Yet Mays' counsel seemed just as impressive as Bonds' slugging display.

A .298 lifetime batting average, 2,935 hits, and a 1.051 career OPS demonstrate that Bonds retained what he learned from his father and godfather and anybody else. "The one thing that people do not see about Barry is that he's an unbelievable tactician," Will Clark said. He recalled benefiting from Bonds' expertise during 1993, their lone season together in San Francisco. Clark struggled to find a prolonged groove that season, batting .283—his second-lowest single-season average—with 14 homers and 73 RBIs. By contrast, Bonds had an electrifying year, which he finished with a .336 average, 46 homers, 123 RBIs, and his third MVP award. At one juncture during that season, Clark grew weary of hooking line drives foul into the right-field seats and approached Bonds to ask him how he kept similar drives fair. The next day, Bonds met Clark for a few extra-special rounds of early batting practice and imparted a mechanical tip. Clark didn't specify what Bonds told him, but admitted, "I used that the rest of my career until I retired."

Here's a theory: Bonds was so feared as a hitter, which caused him to draw so many intentional or semi-intentional walks, that he could have played a year or two after his hitting skills deserted him. With all those free passes he drew, nobody would have discovered right away that he was finished! This actually happened to another all-time great. Check Mickey Mantle's walk totals and lofty on-base percentages for his final four seasons.

Bonds' constant excellence could have won him the same legion of admirers that followed Mays into his retirement. "Barry wanted to be as good as Willie Mays," said right-hander Jeff Brantley, whose dressing stall at Candlestick was alongside Bonds' in 1993. "That's what he was after. He wanted to hit the ball out of the ballpark; he wanted to be the guy who carried the team. He wanted, every time you played the San Francisco Giants, to be the guy about whom you said, 'I can't let him beat me.' That's what he thrived on. And if you walked him, the better that made him feel."

Bonds' deep understanding of hitting would make him a baseball Einstein under any set of circumstances. "It's cool just to listen to him," shortstop Brandon Crawford said during Bonds' stint as a guest instructor during spring training in 2014.

If Bonds reached out to people, they'd probably embrace him. He showed his caring side at a news conference in Washington, an exercise he performed in 2007 before the opener of each road series as he approached Hank Aaron's home run record of 755. Moments before the first question, Bonds approached a pregnant reporter and sweetly asked her, "When are you due?"

But though Bonds' relationship with the world at large appears to be thawing, it's not officially warm. "I wish he had a better rapport with people," Clark said.

"To be totally honest and blunt, I love Barry to death, but he brought most of it on himself."

Said Brantley, "There were things Barry would do or say that, I don't know that they were truly terrible things, but people perceived it that way. I think if he was just a run-of-the-mill player, I don't know that would have gotten that much attention. But there was so much scrutiny of Bonds. Everybody wants to know why a great player is great. And Bonds was truly great. He was as good of a player as I've ever been around. When you're with Barry every day, you start to get the sense that this guy does have that attitude of confidence. He exudes it. It's almost like he creates a bubble around him, but it's not a bubble that he does just to be hateful. It's a bubble to protect himself so he can do what he's supposed to do. I think when you really get down to it, ultimately, in the long run, he's a very misunderstood person."

Aurilia vividly recalled the summer of 2003, when Bonds would stay by his dying father's bedside as long as possible before heading to AT&T Park.

"Everybody always wants to make him out as the bad guy and as the villain," Aurilia said. "When you see the other side of it, you kind of understand it in a different light."

Bobby Bonds' drinking problems, which are well documented, further reveal how Barry's attitude was shaped. "I think if people knew how he was raised in the game and the tougher childhood he had because of a lot of his dad's issues with alcohol, I think people would understand more why he was maybe not as approachable or giddy or happy at times," Aurilia said. "Barry, if you get him one-on-one, could be very engaging and very knowledgeable about the game and could talk to you for a long time about it. But going through those years with him where he's chasing records and seeing that everybody always wants something from you—everybody wants to knock you down. Everybody's trying to say negative things about you. You almost feel sorry for the guy at times, for what he had to go through. Put yourself in that situation. Listen, the guy was getting death threats when he was chasing the home-run record. It's a position I don't think the casual fan can understand because all they see is the highlights and the money and the home runs and the big lifestyle. You don't see the other side of it.

"And I don't think to an extent that I even know the whole part of it. I still talk to him every once in a while. I got along great with him. But he doesn't let a lot of people in, and I think I was one of the few that he actually kind of let in. I never wanted anything from the guy. I never asked him for anything. I just went about my business and played the game. And I think he respected that."

F. Scott Fitzgerald wrote, "There are no second acts in American lives." One gets the sense that Barry Bonds could disprove that. If so, it very well might turn out to be his greatest achievement of all.

CHAPTER 6
2012

Amid the happy mayhem of the visitors' clubhouse at Detroit's Comerica Park, Giants right-hander Sergio Romo placed a phone call to his father, Frank. Romo had just sealed San Francisco's 2012 World Series sweep of the Detroit Tigers by striking out slugger Miguel Cabrera with an 89-mph fastball to conclude the Giants' 4–3, 10-inning victory in Game 4. It would have been an unchallenging pitch under most circumstances. But given the way Romo set it up, it came as a total surprise to Cabrera, who won the first of back-to-back AL Most Valuable Player awards that year.

Savoring his moment of triumph, Romo had a simple reminder for his dad: *I told you so.*

Frank Romo steeped his son in baseball. Not that this required much effort. Frank did not push Sergio into baseball as much as he dangled it in front of him, figuratively speaking. Baby Sergio grabbed it—he got his first glove at age two, before he was out of diapers—and never let the game go.

The Romos' baseball passion proved to be hereditary. Frank, a hard-hitting infielder, drove from the family's home in Brawley, California, to Mexicali, Mexico, about 20 minutes south, to play virtually year-round in an amateur league on Sundays. Sergio was his constant companion.

"Watching my dad play, I wanted to play because he was good," Sergio said. "But I also wanted to play because I thought it was fun. And I still think it's fun."

Playing catch, that classic father-son activity, provided another method of sharing the joys of baseball.

"There was nothing else I wanted to do but play ball with my dad," Sergio said. "I was that kid who, when he'd get home from work and before he had a chance to sit down, go, 'Hey, let's play catch.' He wanted to be out there as much as I did, if not more. He would always say, 'All right, let's go.' It was almost as if he saved a little bit of his energy for me, knowing that I was going to be waiting for him."

Flinging a baseball back and forth was far from idle activity for the younger Romo, who rehearsed performing his fondest dreams.

Said Sergio, "I was that little kid telling my dad, 'Game 7 of the World Series, bottom of the ninth, bases loaded, up by one.' Telling myself it's Mark McGwire in the box. It's Ken Griffey Jr."

In 2012, an aspiring youth might have fantasized about blowing away Miguel Cabrera. Detroit's No. 3 hitter became the first player in 45 years to win the Triple Crown, leading the AL in home runs (44), RBIs (139), and batting average (.330). His OPS (on-base plus slugging percentage) exceeded 1.000 the previous two seasons, a level reserved for the game's elite hitters. Cabrera's OPS sagged in 2012— all the way to .999.

Thus, Sergio Romo earned the right to crow after joining the ranks of elite closers (by Brian Wilson's definition).

"It felt really, really good to call my dad and say, 'I told you so. I told you I was going to do this. I *told* you in the backyard.' It wasn't to prove him wrong. It wasn't to make him feel bad. It wasn't that he made a mistake. It was, 'Remember? I told you, I swore that I was going to do this.'"

As Romo related, his dad's reaction was simple.

"You told me so many times," Frank Romo said.

* * *

Repetition was central to the Giants' 2012 postseason. But it wasn't as if the same things happened over and over, except the results. Winning by margins big and small, emphasizing pitching as well as hitting, the Giants won six consecutive games when facing potential elimination from the same postseason. That matched a standard set by the 1985 Kansas City Royals.

The streak started after the Giants lost their first two Division Series games to Cincinnati by a combined score of 14–2. With the next three games scheduled for Cincinnati, the Reds clearly owned a significant edge. But the Giants believed that playing on the road actually would help rather than hamper them.

"We obviously were not in a good spot, but we were in a better spot mentally going over there than I thought we would be when we were down 0–2," right-hander Ryan Vogelsong said. "As much as we love playing at home, I thought the best thing for us at that point was to go on the road. We had played pretty well on the road all year [the Giants were the NL's highest-scoring team away from home], and I think we put a whole lot of pressure on ourselves those first two games because we were at home and everyone was making a big deal of, you know, you have to win these two because you're going to Cincinnati where they haven't lost three in a row all year. I think at that point in time, our team tried to do way too much those first two games. I think getting on that airplane together and flying across the country allowed everyone time to think and go, what are we doing? Let's just play our game."

To reinforce that, manager Bruce Bochy felt compelled to gather his players before Game 3 and share the biblical tale of Gideon, the military leader who led a vastly outnumbered army of 300 men to victory. As players later said, they appreciated the meaning of Bochy's message, but they truly responded to right fielder Hunter Pence's exhortation. "I love playing with you guys," said Pence, who was acquired from Philadelphia at the July 31 Trade Deadline. Due to his ardor, Pence added, he wasn't ready to quit playing yet and vowed to give his all to guarantee that the Giants' season would continue.

"I still get chills when I think about him giving his speech," said Vogelsong, San Francisco's Game 3 starter. "It was just more of what we talked about on the airplane and on the bus on the way to Cincinnati.

Basically, he said what we were all thinking and talking about. He had tears running down his face because he was that fired up about what he was saying. I'm sure it affected everyone in that room in a different way. But I know for me, I was ready to run through the wall as soon as he got done talking. I kind of took it on myself as, 'You have to throw out a great start and let these boys play some baseball.' For me, it was awesome."

Doubly motivated, the Giants triumphed in 10 innings 2–1. They won despite scoring their first run without benefit of a hit and mustering one hit in nine innings. Moreover, they broke a 10th-inning tie when an eight-time Gold Glove–winning third baseman, Scott Rolen, committed an error and a catcher who was charged with three passed balls all year, Ryan Hanigan, made a fourth. "One of the craziest games of our entire postseason," said Vogelsong, who received support in the second inning when Pence slid to catch Hanigan's liner in foul territory. "That kind of changed my momentum for me on the mound," said Vogelsong, who yielded one run and three hits in five innings. "I don't know if it's baseball luck, but I think sometimes it's just your time."

San Francisco routed Cincinnati in Game 4 8–3 as Angel Pagan lashed the first leadoff homer in Giants postseason history. That preceded San Francisco's 6–4 triumph in the Game 5 clincher. With Pence's rallying cry echoing in their skulls—"Look into each other's eyes! Play for each other! Win each moment! Win each inning!"—the Giants repelled the Reds at every major juncture.

First, Buster Posey delivered a grand slam off Giants nemesis Mat Latos, highlighting a fifth inning in which San Francisco scored all of its runs. Watching from the visitors' bullpen in Great American Ball Park alongside Madison Bumgarner and Jeremy Affeldt, Vogelsong yelled, "Get on the backside of one here, Buster. Drive something." Said Vogelsong years later, "I didn't care if it went out of the ballpark, in the gap, whatever. I just kept on saying, 'Get on the backside of one.'

Right-hander Sergio Romo unleashes a cathartic whoop of joy after striking out Detroit slugger Miguel Cabrera to seal the Giants' 2012 World Series triumph.

Affeldt and Bum weren't saying a whole lot, just kind of watching. And WHACK. As soon as he hit it, it was just a matter of how far it was going to go. I remember Bum and Affeldt saying, 'You called it! You called it!' I said, 'I didn't call homer; I just wanted him to hit the crap out of it.'

"I don't want to say there was the sense of a weight being lifted off our shoulders, but it's like prizefighters feeling each other out for a couple of rounds and then all of a sudden, somebody takes a right hand, and you say, 'Okay, here we go.' I felt like Buster's grand slam was the right hand that broke the ice."

Then Romo survived his first extended confrontation of this postseason, a ninth-inning faceoff with Cincinnati's Jay Bruce.

With two runners on base and one out, Bruce represented the potential winning run. The count ran full, but Bruce kept fouling off Romo's deliveries. Romo finally coaxed a harmless fly ball to left field with his 12th pitch of the at-bat, a slider. That's typically Romo's best pitch, but he also had his sinking fastball working at this particular time. The two-pitch combination proved effective.

"I was trying to keep the ball in the yard, trying to keep it down and away," Romo said. "If he was going to beat me, he wasn't going to beat me with his strengths. He was going to beat me with my strengths."

Javy Lopez, the lefty-on-lefty specialist who retired Bruce on a ground ball to open the eighth inning, admired Romo's work as he watched from the dugout. "He just took over," Lopez said. "That's a credit to him and his ability, not to shy away from a big stage."

After experiencing such a riveting series, the Giants could have regarded the NL Championship Series against the St. Louis Cardinals almost as an anticlimax. And the Giants initially performed as if that were the case, losing three of the first four games. San Francisco looked particularly vulnerable in Game 4, falling 8–3 as Tim Lincecum, who was dropped from the postseason rotation but excelled in a relief role, got the start and worked 4⅔ dull innings. St. Louis outhit the Giants 12–6, and appeared on the verge of capturing the first-ever LCS clash between the previous two World Series winners.

Again backed into a win-or-go-home predicament, the Giants turned to Barry Zito, whose regular season performance was his best since he signed his seven-year, $126 million deal before the 2007 campaign. Not only did he finish 15–8, but the Giants also won his last 11 regular season starts.

The Giants could have assigned the start to Madison Bumgarner, who had received his usual four days' rest. But though the 23-year-old won 16 games that year to share the team lead with Matt Cain, he remained prone to flying frighteningly off-course on occasion. From poor mechanics to insufficient velocity, nothing was going right for Bumgarner, who lost his first two starts of this postseason. He allowed four runs and seven hits in 4⅓ innings in Game 2 of the Division Series against Cincinnati, then coughed up six runs and eight hits in 3⅔ innings in the NLCS opener. Pressure wasn't bothering Bumgarner at all. He proved in 2010, when he blanked Texas on three hits for eight innings in Game 4 of the World Series, that he relished playing for higher stakes. He simply hadn't developed the consistency that would catapult him to October greatness two years hence.

For now, Zito gave the Giants more than enough. He blanked St. Louis for 7⅔ innings, surrendering five hits while striking out six. He also retired 14 of the final 16 Cardinals he faced, including 11 in a row during that stretch. For good measure, he contributed a bunt single that punctuated San Francisco's four-run fourth inning. The Giants won 5–0 to force the series back to San Francisco.

"That day when he walked in the clubhouse, he just had a different look about him," Vogelsong said of Zito. "I can remember saying to

Javy Lopez, 'If this is a good look, we're in business. Because this dude is locked and loaded.'"

Asked about his "game face" and whether it reflected any extra resolve, Zito said, "My only resolve was to do the absolute best I could do. And I think that was a different resolve because I had been in and out of being so wrapped up in results and making sure I could deliver and I think I just decided that I don't give a shit about results today. I just want to give everything I can and do my best, however the chips fall. For me, it took a lot of courage to do that and not get wrapped up in the high stakes and the pressure and what everyone else was worried about that day."

Purging himself of mental burdens allowed Zito to dwell in the realm of the physical.

"I think your mechanics follow your mindset. So when you're relaxed, attacking the zone, worried about one task and keeping everything simple, your body's loose and tension-free and everything seems to be clicking," Zito said. "It's when you're putting too much pressure on yourself to execute that you start getting tension in your body and everything else starts going out the window."

St. Louis still led the series 3–2, but an undercurrent of inevitability seemed to be transporting the Giants and washing away any shortcomings they might have had. Zito's effort was that powerful.

"I felt like Barry gave us the blueprint that night on how to beat them," Vogelsong said. "You have to come out aggressive, pound the strike zone and get some outs early. That's what we did in Games 5 through 7."

The combined score of those games was San Francisco 20, St. Louis 1.

Game 6 was no contest after the Giants piled up four runs in the second inning. The biggest hit in that uprising was a two-run double by second baseman Marco Scutaro, another key Trade Deadline acquisition like Pence. Scutaro's playing status for this series had been jeopardized in Game 2 when St. Louis' Matt Holliday slid ferociously into him in an attempt to break up a double play. Scutaro sustained no structural damage to his left leg and hip, but at 5'10" and 185 pounds, he faced a physical disadvantage when the 6'4", 220-pound Holliday crashed into him.

Citing the discovery of "weaknesses in location" for many of St. Louis' hitters, Vogelsong struck out a career-high nine in seven innings as the Giants won Game 6 6–1. Matt Cain sustained the starters' excellence with a 5⅔-inning stint as the Giants captured the Game 7 clincher 9–0. Fittingly enough, Pence the Preacher provided San Francisco's biggest hit, a three-run double in the second inning that hit his shattered bat three times but was allowable under baseball's rules.

Shortly before Cain left the game, he made sure to leave his imprint on it by hitting Holliday with a pitch to lead off the sixth as rain drenched AT&T Park. Fully comprehending baseball's unwritten rules of retribution, Holliday trotted to first base without even glancing at Cain. Meanwhile, Scutaro reveled in the Giants' impending triumph as he manned his position by happily leaning back between pitches and allowing the rain to cascade into his mouth.

* * *

Most pundits believed that the AL champion Detroit Tigers would subdue the Giants. The Tigers amassed 163 regular season home runs, compared with the Giants' 103.

The Series indeed began with a shower of power. Except it flowed from the bat rack of the Giants, not the Tigers. Playing with something to prove, Pablo Sandoval tied a record shared by Babe Ruth, Reggie

Jackson, and Albert Pujols by smashing three home runs—including two off Detroit ace Justin Verlander—in San Francisco's 8–3 victory. This was the same Sandoval whose postseason activity was extremely limited in 2010 because he was overweight. These days, Sandoval was hardly svelte, but he remained quick and nimble around the bag. And though his regular season batting average dropped from .315 in 2011 to .283, nothing was fundamentally wrong with his swing.

A factor to bear in mind (in Sandoval's case, that bear's a Kung Fu Panda, his old nickname): Home runs usually don't come in bunches at AT&T Park. Only 84 homers were hit there in 2012, by far the majors' lowest total.

But, as Vogelsong said, "For a guy who gets to see Pablo every day, there was no surprise factor in what he did at all. The one thing I always loved about Pablo was, I felt like the situation was never too big for him. The big stage was not the big stage. It was just another game at 7:05. Obviously the whole world saw that."

Which, in turn, galvanized the Giants. "I was probably as fired up as I've ever been for a game that I wasn't playing in—watching history and watching this guy do things that not a whole lot of people could do," Vogelsong said.

The so-called experts dismissed the Game 1 pitching matchup, with Zito opposing reigning American League Cy Young Award winner Justin Verlander, as heavily stacked in Detroit's favor. It was indeed a mismatch, but not the kind most people anticipated. While Sandoval's slugging helped limit Verlander to four innings, Zito allowed one run and six hits in 5⅔ innings before Lincecum struck out five in 2⅓ perfect innings of relief.

Zito acknowledged being able to sustain personal momentum from his previous outing. "Essentially, I had this really great experience in St. Louis, just keeping things as simple as possible, giving everything I had on every pitch, and really trying to stay with the fundamentals and keep things simple," he said. "And not get caught up in the whole drama and the whole story and Verlander and everything else, which is very difficult to do. But it was something I was able to do—probably not as well as I did in St. Louis, but it was something I was able to do well enough. Certainly all the runs off Verlander were very helpful."

Asked whether he felt any irony about being asked to start two of the season's biggest games after not even having a chance to pitch in the 2010 postseason, Zito focused on 2012 and the attitude adjustment he was able to make after a subpar Game 4 start in the Division Series at Cincinnati (two runs and four hits allowed along with four walks in a no-decision).

"It was such an interesting experience for me, because I had pitched in Cincinnati and that was when I put too much pressure on myself," he said. "I did want to bring it home, so to speak, for the fans and everyone else who had something to do with bringing me over to San Francisco and I wanted to prove that I could get it done in the playoffs and all that and I put all that and I did so poorly—no surprise; that's what happens when athletes try to do too much. That's why in my experience in St. Louis, I was able to do the complete opposite mentally and not be attached to anything—and at the end of the day, really not even care what anybody thought about me. That was between me and God, essentially. I felt like I was put in a place to have an opportunity to do everything I could do and I was so grateful for the opportunity."

In Game 2, Bumgarner regained his form and lasted seven innings to generate San Francisco's 2–0 victory. He reversed his fortunes while yielding two hits, walking two, and striking out eight. A simple change in the arm angle of Bumgarner's throwing motion, suggested by pitching coach Dave Righetti and bullpen coach Mark Gardner, made all the difference, though Bumgarner's innate adaptability helped.

Said Vogelsong, "Bum will decide he's going to change his mechanics on Tuesday when he's pitching on Thursday and he'll be able to do it." Even, as Bumgarner demonstrated, under pressurized circumstances such as the World Series. As Vogelsong said, "It's not just a Sunday afternoon in St. Louis."

It was a Saturday evening in Detroit when Vogelsong's turn to pitch arrived in Game 3. He habitually refrained from speaking to reporters two days before he pitched, but this time Major League Baseball protocol demanded his participation in a news conference on the afternoon before the game. Vogelsong cooperated admirably. Nevertheless, shortly after Vogelsong entered the interview room, an MLB.com colleague seated next to me took a look at the pitcher's intense visage, which appeared to be carved from stone. My obviously shocked co-worker leaned over and whispered, "Does he *always* look like that?" I pondered the question for a millisecond. "Pretty much," I responded.

Game-time temperature at Comerica Park was 47 degrees, which seemed to mute the offense for both teams. As big a game as it was, the details of the Giants' scoring haven't been carved in immortality. Pence drew a leadoff walk in the second inning from Detroit starter Anibal Sanchez and scored on Gregor Blanco's triple, which preceded Brandon Crawford's two-out single.

More memorable were the runs that *didn't* score, particularly in the Tigers' half of the fifth inning when they loaded the bases with one out. Vogelsong approached escape by striking out Quintin Berry, but one extremely formidable challenge loomed: Cabrera, who could turn the entire World Series in Detroit's favor with one swing. Fortunately for the Giants, Vogelsong was ready.

"For some reason, even the night before and the whole day, I had a feeling that I was going to have an at-bat with him at some point that was going to mean something," Vogelsong said. As he and Posey discussed before the game how they'd approach Detroit's hitters, Vogelsong articulated the merits of using the pitch that he believed would work the best against Cabrera—an inside, sinking fastball—but only sparingly.

"I had gotten him out 'in' in the past," said Vogelsong, who had limited Cabrera to one hit in five at-bats. "So I knew he knew I was probably going to come in on him at some point. But I wanted to try to save it as long as I could."

Vogelsong heeded this plan and began the game throwing Cabrera soft stuff outside. Cabrera stroked a first-inning single on a curveball, but Vogelsong held Detroit scoreless as Prince Fielder grounded into a double play. When Cabrera led off the fourth, Vogelsong said, "I threw him change-ups away and I left one over the middle of the plate and he hit it about 460 feet foul in the upper deck. Then I threw him another one right after that, broke his bat and he hit a little flare to second base."

Thus, Vogelsong felt no apprehension when he confronted Cabrera in the fifth. "When he came up in that spot, I knew exactly what I wanted to do and I knew I had set it up the whole game, because I had stayed away from him, hard-soft-away, hard-soft-away," he said. "I didn't know what the result was going to be, but I was pretty confident about throwing the ball 'in' to him in that at-bat."

Vogelsong courted danger by not throwing his first pitch to Cabrera as far inside as he wanted. Demonstrating a true run producer's knack for making any contact necessary to drive in his teammates, Cabrera hit a ball down the right-field line that landed foul. It would have cleared the bases had it landed a few feet in the other direction. Undaunted, Posey called for another sinker inside, which Cabrera popped up to shortstop. "It was crazy that came to pass, because that's exactly what I thought was going to happen the night before," Vogelsong said.

Footnote: Vogelsong believed that striking out Berry was the inning's most critical moment. "Since there was only one out, he didn't even have to get a hit for them to score a run. So I felt like his at-bat was bigger, especially because he was left-handed and lefties were a little bit tougher for me than righties. I actually made two mistakes in the at-bat that he fouled straight back and then I snuck a heater by him to strike him out." After Vogelsong lasted 5⅔ innings, Lincecum contributed 2⅓ innings of smothering relief before Romo pitched a perfect ninth to conclude San Francisco's 2–0 win. It was the Giants' fourth shutout of the postseason, equaling a record shared by the 2010 club.

* * *

San Francisco owned a commanding 3–0 Series lead. But that edge looked a lot less lopsided with some very conceivable worst-case-scenario logic applied.

For instance, assume that the Tigers could win Game 4. Then they'd have Verlander, the AL's reigning Cy Young Award winner, starting at home in an extremely winnable game. And suppose the Tigers indeed win that one. Then the Giants lead by a bare 3–2 margin, with Detroit's momentum blunting their home-field advantage.

So the Giants had to win Game 4 to avoid a lot of fuss.

They did so by receiving efficient pitching from Matt Cain and the bullpen, along with just enough offense. Cabrera finally hit his inevitable homer, a two-run drive in the third inning that put the Tigers ahead 2–1. The Giants inched ahead on Posey's two-run homer in the sixth off Max Scherzer. Then Delmon Young homered in Detroit's half of the inning to tie the score, which was how matters remained until the 10th.

Ryan Theriot, San Francisco's primary second baseman until he was displaced by Scutaro's arrival in the Trade Deadline deal with Colorado, capped his surprise start as the designated hitter by delivering a lead-off single. Presented with a difficult task as a left-handed batter facing a

131

left-handed pitcher, Brandon Crawford executed his duties perfectly by laying down a sacrifice bunt that advanced Theriot to second base. Up came Scutaro, who amassed 44 RBIs in 61 regular season games before winning Most Valuable Player honors in the NLCS by tying a record with 14 hits. Given Scutaro's seemingly ceaseless productivity, his RBI single was completely unsurprising.

Entrusted with the lead, Romo fanned Austin Jackson and Don Kelly. The next batter—how could it be any different?—was Cabrera. On the mound, Romo was thinking, *Go figure, it would be you*. Revisiting the moment four years later, Romo said, "It wasn't necessarily David versus Goliath, but that was the mentality we took. Here I am with my slingshot. It's hard not to have that respect. But at the same time, it's 'Okay, let's do it. He ain't never seen me before.'"

Aware that he couldn't fool a hitter of Cabrera's quality, Romo threw five consecutive sliders, adhering to the closer's credo of refusing to get beat with anything less than your best pitch. After Cabrera fouled off the fifth pitch to keep the count 2–2, Posey reasoned that the slugger had seen enough sliders to help him establish his timing. So Posey changed course by calling for a fastball. "Okay, cool," Romo thought. "I think Buster and I were probably the only ones in the whole world who knew that we were throwing the fastball there. In my head, I said, 'Just hit the glove.'"

Using a four-seam grip, Romo did just that. An instant later, he was treated to the sight of a wild-eyed Posey rushing to the mound to envelop him in the hug that would begin a spirited celebration.

"When I threw the strike and he caught it, there was a moment there where I paused," Romo said. "I didn't know what to do, because I didn't know what happened."

Romo quickly grasped the meaning of the moment. "I was a part of something that was way bigger than myself," he said.

CHAPTER 7
CANDLESTICK

The flaws of Candlestick Park, the Giants' home from 1960 to '99, were obvious. But the wind couldn't blow away the memories minted there. The chill didn't cool the passion of the fans who braved the elements. Candlestick was inadequate—that's a nice word for a "dump"—and had to be abandoned. But as proved by its refusal to crack during the 1989 Loma Prieta earthquake, it was built to last. Candlestick thus preserved countless lives, including mine. Mostly, it was a place where people learned to love the game, creating allegiances and generating pure fun that will reside forever in hearts and souls. Including mine. Giants pitching coach Dave Righetti, who grew up in San Jose, got it right when he said, "To me, it was the greatest stadium in the world. Because it was where the Giants played."

It was where I experienced that wholly American rite of passage: Going with Dad to my first ballgame. The date was May 24, 1969, the Pittsburgh Pirates provided the opposition and I was a week short of my 10th birthday. We sat in the upper deck behind first base. It's extremely corny and exceedingly cliché to say so, but the field was the most beautiful thing I had ever seen, and I didn't know the sun could shine so brightly. This was love at first sight. Bobby Bonds homered in the first inning and Willie McCovey homered four innings later. Mike McCormick pitched a complete game in a 5–2 Giants victory. There was no turning back. I was *hooked*.

It was where the importance of being a gentleman was reaffirmed. About an hour before a Saturday afternoon game against the Cubs, I trudged through the main concourse back toward my seat in mild dejection because I failed to get Ernie Banks' autograph, though he had signed for an ample amount of time. Suddenly I noticed Sandy Koufax, NBC's analyst on its backup Game of the Week telecasts, striding toward a ramp to the press level. Others saw him, too, and we quickly surrounded him. Since this was an era when most kids still had manners, we said, "Mr. Koufax, may we please have your autograph?" "Sure thing, boys," the great man said. "I just gotta keep moving." I distinctly recall that Mr. Koufax didn't have a hair out of place, and having just undergone a growth spurt, I was nearly as tall as him.

It was where I learned that, in baseball, anything truly is possible. On Labor Day 1973, I watched the Giants fall behind the Dodgers 8–1 before rallying for six runs in the seventh inning. Los Angeles' defense botched a pair of sacrifice-bunt attempts by the Giants in the ninth, setting up Bobby Bonds' game-winning grand slam. Final score: Giants 11, Dodgers 8. Compiling a list of my all-time favorite games would be challenging, but I know that this one would be a finalist.

It was where I reveled even in the sights and sounds of the vendors. There was the elderly African American gentleman, always smiling, who sold programs before the game and peanuts in the late innings. A balding, robust-looking fellow roamed the grandstand and repeated his distinctive call: "BEEEEER! Bottle o' BEEEEER! Ice-cold bottle o' BEEEEER..." Another guy sold a variety of goods but never varied the sequence in which he hawked them: "Hats! Bats! Pennants! Baseballs!" During a junior varsity basketball game in my sophomore year against Woodrow Wilson High School (since closed), something about the face of the substitute I was assigned to guard nagged me. I plumbed my memory and solved my personal mystery before the final buzzer sounded. Encountering my opponent in the postgame handshake line, I exclaimed, "You sell malts at Candlestick!" He laughed and acknowledged his identity.

None of these games or events is unique to Candlestick. Similar occurrences have happened everywhere else in baseball.

Nor is my Candlestick upbringing all that unique. Giants president and CEO Larry Baer's destiny took root there. A fourth-generation San Franciscan, Baer and his father, Monroe, were frequent visitors to the yard, favoring Saturday afternoon games. During baseball season, young Larry waited expectantly on Thursdays or Fridays for his father to return home from his downtown law office with the treasured tickets that he typically purchased at a Roos-Atkins men's clothing store ("Roos-Atkins will suit you" was among the establishment's advertising slogans of the period). The Baers preferred public transportation and would board the Municipal Railway's 28 Ballpark Express bus, which led them down 19th Avenue to Candlestick. They liked sitting down the right-field line, in lower reserved sections 19 or 21, because the sun shone there for most of the afternoon. Purchasing hot dogs, which the vendors slathered with Gulden's mustard by using wooden sticks that resembled oversized tongue depressors, was an essential part of the ballpark experience. One fine Saturday in the late 1960s, Jack Hiatt, the Giants' cheerful backup catcher, tossed a baseball to young Larry, who guarded it like the Hope Diamond on the bus ride back home. Hiatt had a long stint as the Giants' player development director and still serves as a player personnel advisor.

"I literally had the Giants in my blood almost since Day 1," Baer said.

Make no mistake, however. Candlestick was something else.

"It was a ballpark like no other," said left-hander Shawn Estes, who pitched for the Giants from 1995 to 2001. "There's no comparison to it in all of baseball."

The wind gave Candlestick its identity.

"You'd see infielders' caps blow off and get pinned on the center-field fence within three seconds," said Will Clark. "You'd look at the flagpoles in center field and all of the flags would be blowing at one another. You'd be in the batter's box trying to pick up the baseball in the middle of 50 hot-dog wrappers blowing around in a little mini-tornado right in front of home plate."

Hiatt, whose Giants career spanned 1965–69, played at Candlestick before upper-deck seating became completely encircled to accommodate the arrival of the 49ers in 1971. Fans purchasing ordinarily desirable seats behind first base did so at their own peril. "I felt so bad for them," Hiatt said. "Sand would start blowing off the infield and kill those people."

Before night games, players could set their watches according to the wind, which regularly began its initial onslaught between 5:00 and 5:30 PM. One day, the strength of the gusts had an unusual effect on Candlestick's batting cage, a clunky contraption that prompted Hiatt to say, "I think they made it out of a World War I tank. It took a tractor to move that thing." However, Mother Nature jumped behind the wheel on this particular afternoon. Said Hiatt, "The wind blew the cage over the end of the mound past the right of second base, all the way to the right-center-field fence."

Extreme conditions, from the high sky to low fog, threatened to influence the outcome of numerous games.

"First base, second base, and right field was a sun field," Clark said. "So when the ball went up, everybody had to put gloves up [to shade their eyes] and glasses down."

Former shortstop Rich Aurilia, who reached the majors with the Giants in 1995, diplomatically said, "You always have good memories with your first ballpark that you get to in the big leagues." Aurilia also recalled, "I remember one time it was so foggy that somebody had to go out in the middle of the game and hit a fly ball with a fungo to see if the outfielders could see it, to decide if we would continue the game."

Dodgers shortstop Maury Wills, who played 103 games at Candlestick in his long career, pointed out that the combination of sun and wind proved treacherous for infielders. "Usually when a pop fly went up high, nobody actually wanted it, even though it might be in your area," he said.

Candlestick just happened to be built in what might be the coldest part of San Francisco, where above-average temperatures usually don't materialize until mid-September, a period known as "Indian Summer." Second baseman Jeff Kent, who won the National League Most Valuable Player Award with the Giants in 2000, recalled commuting from Foster City, a suburb located 12 miles south of San Francisco, to Candlestick.

"The temperature would drop 20 degrees," Kent said.

This necessitated adjustments in baseball apparel. Long underwear was a common accessory at Candlestick. Also, Willie McCovey said, "They used to have this hot Vaseline—we just called it 'Hot Stuff'— that you put all over your body. Actually, you would burn up if you put too much of it on. So you could put on only a little bit of that stuff. It kept you warm underneath."

Giants bench coach Ron Wotus cited a side effect of the high winds and low temperatures. "You had to deal with the infield drying out," said Wotus, who joined the major league staff in 1998, the Giants' next-to-last year at Candlestick. "That could get rough at times."

One Giant made defense look easy. Willie Mays always seemed to beat the ball to where it would land, between the gaps and from shallow center field to the wall. Candlestick's capricious conditions, said Hiatt, "made a lot of people look stupid. And Willie played it like it was nothing. *Nothing!*"

For hitters, however, the wind was universally cruel. It required nothing less than total focus. "To a certain extent, it made you a better ballplayer because no matter what was going on around you, you still had to concentrate on your job and concentrate on the baseball," Clark said. "As a hitter, because of the wind blowing so much, if you did not hit a line drive, you were pretty much guaranteed you were not going to get a base hit. So you really had to concentrate on what you were doing and get to know your craft."

Completed in 1960, Candlestick Park was the place everybody loved to hate, largely because of its bone-chilling breezes. But it held up admirably during the 1989 Loma Prieta earthquake.

Mays lost a countless number of home runs by pulling pitches into Candlestick's crosswind. "I can remember so many balls that went into left-center field that turned out to be dying quails. These were balls that would have gone out of any other ballpark," said Ken Henderson, a Giants outfielder from 1965 to '72. "Because of the wind, they were held up and caught. Which made his statistics even more incredible, I think."

A baseball genius, Mays became adept at stroking pitches to right-center field. During the 12 full seasons he played at Candlestick (1960–71), he hit more homers there (202) than on the road (194).

McCovey, who played more games (1,086) than anyone at Candlestick, also endured his share of bad luck by pulling pitches down the right-field line that would get blown foul. More often, McCovey's swing was the stronger force. He hit more homers at Candlestick (236) than anyone. "That's one thing I'm kind of proud of," he said.

Had Candlestick been a leaving, breathing entity, it would have been proud of its impregnability through the Loma Prieta quake. Ceremonies preceding Game 3 of the Giants–A's World Series were about to begin when, at 5:04 PM, an earthquake measuring 6.9 on the Richter scale shook the entire Bay Area for about 15 seconds.

Those were the longest 15 seconds of my life, which I thought was about to end as I struggled to stay composed in the auxiliary press section, located behind home plate in Candlestick's upper deck. I watched the light towers sway and the field undulate. Giants right-hander-turned-broadcaster Mike Krukow compared the latter to "a 600-pound gopher going 40 miles an hour under my feet."

Clark watched the San Andreas Fault slip before his eyes. "I had just gotten through running a sprint to center field," he said. "I was walking back towards the right-field line. And I could see it coming. You could actually see the wave coming through the stands."

Fans briefly celebrated once the shaking stopped. "A big roar went up from the stands," Krukow said. "The attitude was basically, 'All right, now we're gonna rock the A's.' People were psyched. They were into the whole deal."

Nobody knew yet that a significant portion of the Nimitz Freeway in Oakland and part of the Bay Bridge had collapsed, or that fires would erupt in San Francisco's Marina District. The game was postponed. The Series, which Oakland ultimately swept, didn't resume until 10 days later on October 27.

Through it all, Candlestick proved heroic. Except for a few relatively small concrete hunks that shook loose, the edifice remained intact. Tens of thousands of people remained unharmed.

"That could have been catastrophic had one of the sections collapsed," Krukow said.

Until 1997, the first of eight consecutive winning seasons and a span in which they moved to then–Pacific Bell Park, fan support appeared on the brink of collapsing. The Giants took a major step toward saving the franchise for San Francisco in 1978, when they spent 95 days in first place and attendance soared from 700,056 in 1977 to 1,740,477. But attendance declined in five of the next seven years. Hired before the '77 season to run promotions and marketing, Pat Gallagher tried virtually everything to lure people to Candlestick.

Gallagher brought in the cast of *Happy Days*, when the show's popularity was soaring, for a softball game. He hired Karl Wallenda, the famed tightrope walker, to stroll on a high wire between the foul poles in 1977. Once, Gallagher tried to capitalize on the wind by scheduling a kite festival. That was among the few days the Candlestick breezes took a holiday.

Maintaining a sense of humor about the ballpark's weather, Gallagher introduced the "Croix de Candlestick" in 1983, a button that

141

fans received for staying through an entire extra-inning night game. Today, people still show up at AT&T Park with caps or clothing festooned with multiple croix.

"What we were saying was, 'Look, this place sucks,'" Gallagher said. "It didn't make us play any better. It just made people feel better about it."

The Giants finished 66–96 in 1984, the year that the Crazy Crab appeared as the club's antimascot. Aware that many San Francisco fans considered themselves too sophisticated to accept somebody (or something) that was proliferating across the majors like the San Diego Chicken or Mr. Met, the Giants actually encouraged fans to boo the Crab—though management feared for his safety when spectators began throwing hard objects such as bottles or batteries at him.

In 1985, the Giants tried playing a home schedule featuring 63 day games. "Real grass. Real sunshine. Real baseball." They got two out of three right, as the Giants lost 100 games for the first and only time in their history.

The Giants nearly moved to Toronto, Denver, and Tampa–St. Petersburg before the Peter Magowan–led ownership group took over the team in the 1992–93 offseason. Magowan and Baer, then executive vice president, devised a plan for winning an election—the team had lost four of them—that would enable the franchise to build the ballpark it currently occupies.

As for Candlestick, one almost expects to see it still looming by the bayside after passing the Brisbane exit on Highway 101. Though Candlestick was dismantled after the 49ers played their final game there in 2013, the memories of what happened there are so strong, it's as if it continues to exist.

It exists for people who got golf-ball-sized goosebumps by watching Mays merely saunter to the on-deck circle, his uniform as elegant as a tuxedo.

It exists for purists who believe that San Francisco's finest spans are the Golden Gate Bridge, the Bay Bridge, and McCovey stretching at first base for a throw.

It exists for anyone who refused to leave his or her seat whenever Clark—that's Jack or Will—was due to bat.

It exists for anybody spellbound by the talents of the Bondses, *pere et fil.*

It exists for anyone who marveled at Marichal kicking his left leg toward those impossibly high light towers in the middle of his marvelous motion.

It exists for anybody who still can summon Jeff Carter's voice in one's internal public-address system.

It exists for anybody who paid 90 cents—*ninety cents*—to sit in the bleachers.

It exists for people who emptied mothballs from their warmest clothes to attend a game in July or August.

It exists for fans who supported John Montefusco, Tim Lincecum, and Madison Bumgarner with equal ardor.

It exists for folks who loved to debate who was the better closer (Rod Beck or Robb Nen) or double-play combination (Chris Speier/ Tito Fuentes or Jose Uribe/Robby Thompson).

It exists for everyone who, however briefly, ignored Candlestick's faults and appreciated the game in front of them.

143

CHAPTER 8
HIS MAGNIFICENCE

Wherever Juan Marichal had gone, it wasn't August 15, 2015. That was the date of an interview I was granted with the legendary right-hander in a press-box office at AT&T Park. Miniature replicas of the Marichal statue that's entrenched by the ballpark's Lefty O'Doul Gate would be given to fans the next day, so he was in town as part of the promotion.

As our chat ended, I offered Marichal copies of two feature stories I wrote about him a handful of years back. He accepted them eagerly, explaining that a young nephew or grandson of his was gathering such articles to put in a collection. I was pleasantly surprised.

That feeling was nothing compared with what I experienced next.

I had something else to show Marichal: a scrapbook I kept from 1969 through the early '70s featuring newspaper clippings of his best games from that portion of his career. The batch of clips, which were arranged randomly, ended with Marichal's election to the Hall of Fame in 1983. Did I exceed the bounds of professionalism? Probably. But I wanted Marichal to know that I appreciated him and his achievements.

I assumed that Marichal would briskly flip through my ragged batch of faded clips and bid me a courteous farewell. I couldn't have been more wrong.

Marichal grew silent as he took my scrapbook and stared at its cover, which I decorated with his page from the 1969 Giants Yearbook. He studied each of my entries as if he were a scholar inspecting the Dead Sea Scrolls. He turned every sheet slowly, even tenderly, like a museum curator inspecting a prized acquisition.

Marichal had entered the Wayback Machine. August 15 no longer existed in his mind.

Marichal's rapturous reaction to my scrapbook astonished me, as if I were 10 years old all over again while he blew away the entire National League. He needed no further affirmation of his greatness. He was enshrined in Cooperstown. He was widely acknowledged as the finest ballplayer ever from the Dominican Republic. A recently published book lionizing his incomparable 16-inning confrontation with Braves left-hander Warren Spahn was in circulation. The Giants had honored Marichal in almost every way possible over the years, from retiring his jersey number 27 to awarding him honorary World Series championship rings to building the statue in his honor.

Yet it almost seemed as if Marichal was just realizing what a marvelous pitcher he was. At least according to my perception. *I really did all this*, he appeared to be thinking. Or, perhaps, my scrapbook revived memories that had lain dormant for several years. Maybe he had bottled up his competitive instincts for such a long time; here, he allowed himself to sniff the cork.

It was easy to imagine Marichal becoming younger with each page he turned. Why not? Though baseball began capturing my imagination late in Marichal's career, I nevertheless managed to preserve a representative sampling of his mastery.

These were among the headlines he scanned:

MARICHAL EARNS 200TH VICTORY

MARICHAL STOPS DODGERS 11–3

JUAN 1-HITS REDS—GIANTS STILL 1/2 BACK

JUAN BLANKS DODGERS; GIANTS 2 1/2 BACK

JUAN'S SHUTOUT PUTS GIANTS IN FIRST

Respecting Marichal's silence—and awe-struck by him as much as I ever was—I intended to keep my mouth shut. But I couldn't restrain myself when he reached a two-page spread I created from the sports section of the May 16, 1971, San Francisco *Examiner*. One day earlier, Marichal limited the Dodgers to six hits in a 1–0 Giants triumph before a standing-room-only audience at Candlestick that included me and much of my fifth-grade class. "That's one of the best games I've ever seen," I murmured. Marichal wore a beatific expression as he lingered briefly on this entry, then carefully turned another page.

Since the door to the room we occupied was closed, I suddenly started to wonder whether members of Marichal's entourage were concerned about his disappearance. His stroll through the past ended soon enough. I felt privileged to open this path.

*　*　*

I was somewhat stunned that nobody else wanted to interview Marichal that afternoon. Then again, he's routinely overlooked.

"He's not given the recognition he deserves," said catcher Jack Hiatt, one of Marichal's contemporaries. "Because he couldn't throw 300 miles an hour, his name doesn't come up. But, buddy, I'm gonna tell you something: You ask any of those hitters that faced him during that era, they didn't want any part of him."

Several accomplished hitters who faced Marichal at his best indeed echoed Hiatt when I spoke with them. Frank Robinson compared Marichal favorably with the aces most often recognized with pitching excellence in the 1960s, Dodgers left-hander Sandy Koufax and Cardinals righty Bob Gibson. Marichal eclipsed both of them as the decade's leading winner, accumulating 191 victories.

"Juan was right up there with them," said Robinson, the only performer to win the Most Valuable Player award in both leagues. "He didn't have to take a back seat."

Joe Torre, who hit .297 in 18 seasons, marveled at Marichal's powers of deception. Marichal could throw a fastball, curveball, screwball, slider, and change-up from three different angles—straight overhand, a three-quarter release point, and sidearm.

"The only thing you knew was that it was going to be over the plate," Torre said. "You didn't know where it was going to come from or which part of the plate it was going to go over. It was remarkable. You could put a postage stamp down there and he could throw the ball over it."

"Once in a while, we looked for him to throw one between his legs," Robinson said. "It wouldn't have been surprising."

Marichal's impossibly high leg kick, which typically prevented hitters from quickly seeing the baseball out of his hand, was essential to his powers of deception.

"Pete Rose asked me once, 'How the hell do you ever hit this guy?'" Hiatt said. "Back then, there was a lot of diversity in deliveries. There were unusual deliveries. And hiding the ball was a key. You couldn't find the ball with Juan because of that high leg kick."

From a purely aesthetic standpoint, Marichal's kick made him extremely fun to watch. Bob Stevens, the eloquent San Francisco *Chronicle* writer who covered Marichal's career, summarized it best with this description: "If you placed all the pitchers in history behind a transparent curtain, where only a silhouette was visible, Juan's high kick motion would be the easiest to identify. He brought to the mound what Van Gogh and Da Vinci brought to the canvas—beauty, individuality and class."

Images of Marichal inspired Dennis Eckersley to develop his own elevated leg kick. "That's totally where I got it," said Eckersley, who won the Cy Young and Most Valuable Player awards in the American League in 1992 before proceeding to the Hall of Fame. "Because I tried to kick my (left) leg up so high, and therefore, I started using my (right) leg (to push off) as a little kid, and that's why I threw so hard. A lot of kids don't use their legs. They never learn that."

As Hiatt indicated, Marichal lacked a truly overpowering fastball. But it was more than functional. "He would dazzle you with off-speed pitches until the count went to 3–2 and then throw the fastball right by you," Hiatt said.

Hall of Fame first baseman Orlando Cepeda recalled a challenging matchup with Milwaukee Braves slugger Eddie Mathews. "Mathews was a great fastball hitter. The bases were loaded with one out," Cepeda said. "Juan told (catcher) Tom Haller, 'I want to throw nothing but fastballs.' Haller said, 'But Matthews is a great fastball hitter.' Juan said, 'Yes, but I'm going to throw it where he isn't going to hit it.'"

Marichal's curveball proved devastating. Hiatt observed with amusement that while other pitchers threw an "Uncle Charlie," the common euphemism for a curveball, Marichal's bender was so good that Larry Jansen, the Giants' pitching coach from 1961 to '71, dubbed it the "Lord Charles," suggesting that it was a cut above almost all others.

If any pitch separated Marichal from other top starters, it was the screwball. Most pitchers didn't, and still don't, even try to throw it. Bent on improving his effectiveness against left-handed batters, Marichal played winter ball during one offseason relatively early in his career to gain command of the screwball, which would break away from lefty hitters and into a right-handed swinger.

"That's the hardest pitch in the world to master," Hiatt said.

Nevertheless, Dodgers first baseman/outfielder Ron Fairly said, "He could throw it at any time, especially when it got down to a 2–2 or a 3–2 count."

Skilled as Marichal was, he remains humble in his self-evaluations. "It was easy to pitch with guys like Willie Mays in center field," he said. "To play with those men—Mays, [Willie] McCovey, Cepeda, Felipe Alou, Gaylord Perry, Tom Haller, Jim Ray Hart, Jim Davenport, Chris Speier, Tito Fuentes, Garry Maddox, Gary Matthews, Bobby Bonds—I

Juan Marichal will always overshadow every Giants pitcher who follows him—quite literally, in this case. William Behrends' superb sculpture captures the Hall of Fame right-hander's signature leg kick.

was thrilled to be on that field with all of them. It was a great honor for me."

The Giants reciprocated by relishing Marichal's appearances. "We knew that was 'win' day when he went out there," said McCovey, the Hall of Fame first baseman.

Speier, who began his 19-year major league playing career with the Giants in 1971, particularly appreciated Marichal. "Juan was gentle and reassuring," said Speier, a three-time All-Star shortstop who's now the Washington Nationals' bench coach. "He was extremely helpful in allowing me to make rookie mistakes and build my confidence by giving me a pat on the fanny when I'd screw up behind him. He kind of took me underneath his wing a little bit. I was a bit overwhelmed and he reassured me that I belonged there. 'Don't worry about the mistakes and I'll pick you up. Be ready for the next one.' He was really great from that standpoint."

Marichal pitched a one-hit shutout against Philadelphia in his major league debut on July 19, 1960. He walked one and struck out 12, displaying the superior control that remained one of his most distinguishing traits. He averaged 21 complete games per season from 1962 to '71, reaching a high of 30 (in 38 starts) in 1968. He won 20 games six times while building a 238–140 record with the Giants. A nine-time All-Star, Marichal ranks as one of the finest performers in Midsummer Classic history, recording an 0.50 ERA (one earned run in 18 innings) spanning eight appearances.

"He was like nobody else," said Steve Stone, the Chicago White Sox television commentator who began his 11-year big league pitching career with the Giants in 1971.

However, statistics fail to measure one of Marichal's most significant deeds: the friendship he ultimately forged with John Roseboro. On August 22, 1965, an enraged Marichal hit the Dodgers catcher over the head with his bat during a third-inning plate appearance, punctuating tension and mutual animosity that had been rising since the game's first pitch. Marichal opened a cut that required 14 stitches to close. The damage to his reputation wouldn't be fixed as easily. Marichal missed election to the Hall of Fame in his first two appearances on the ballot. But Roseboro publicly backed Marichal's Cooperstown candidacy, prompting an instant turnaround in the voting. Not everybody knew that they had settled their differences years earlier. They continued to grow closer, participating in golf tournaments and appearing at various events together before Roseboro died in 2002. Marichal was an honorary pallbearer and speaker at Roseboro's funeral.

Roger Angell wrote that baseball is so intensely remembered because only baseball is so intensely watched. That truism explains my keen recollection of most of the games I saw Marichal pitch. With an assist from Baseball-reference.com to verify a few details, here's a partial list of performances by Marichal that I was lucky enough to witness:

June 13, 1969
Giants 4, Expos 2

My first night game! Paid attendance was a whopping 5,893 on a Friday. My parents and I waltzed up to the box office and bought seats that couldn't have been more than a dozen rows behind home plate. Great for Marichal–watching. As I marveled at his leg kick, he pitched a complete game and basically did what a future Hall of Famer should do to an expansion team in its first year of existence. But the Expos were worth watching, particularly through a 10-year-old kid's eyes. Adolfo Phillips, their leadoff batter, swung so hard in the on-deck circle that I thought he'd injure himself. Rusty Staub threw out a runner at home plate from deep right field. And I liked their tri-colored caps so much that I bought one.

April 25, 1970
Expos 7, Giants 3

This was Marichal's regular season debut following a horrible reaction to a pair of penicillin shots he received after he caught a bad cold during the Giants' ill-advised Spring Training trip to Japan. Still weakened, he somehow managed to pitch five shutout innings, stranding seven base runners. Marichal's ability to excel even without his best stuff taught me how extensive a pitching toolbox he possessed.

May 15, 1971
Giants 1, Dodgers 0

This happened to be Marichal's lone career 1–0 victory over the Dodgers. It was far from his only win against them overall. He posted a 37–18 lifetime record against the Dodgers, reflecting his knack for coming through when the Giants needed him most—that is, against their archrival. Against the Dodgers at Candlestick, Marichal built an unbelievable 21–4 mark. "Juan would elevate his game and mow through that lineup," Hiatt said.

June 18, 1971
Giants 7, Padres 3

Here, in retrospect, was where I learned that Marichal was driven to perfection. He was two outs away from completing a shutout when Cito Gaston belted a three-run homer. I distinctly remember watching Marichal stalk off the mound, bellowing at (I think) nobody in particular. I shared this experience with Giants pitching coach Dave Righetti, who completely understood Marichal's behavior. Righetti pointed out that Marichal probably obsessed over his career and season shutout totals, and might even have had winning the NL's ERA title on his mind. In short, he held himself to a higher standard.

Said Hiatt, "Every game was, to him, a World Series game."

September 10, 1972
Giants 8, Reds 2

I'm fairly certain that Marichal pitched with a mild abdominal strain that forced him to abandon his signature leg kick temporarily. Though Marichal pitched seven solid innings and beat the Big Red Machine, watching him perform without his high kick was like celebrating Christmas without Santa Claus (I ceased believing in Santa long before then, but you know what I mean).

This demonstrated the athleticism required to perform the leg kick. "Guys would pull a hamstring if they did that now," Hiatt said.

July 15, 1973
Giants 12, Pirates 0

In Marichal's 52nd and final career shutout, he again subdued a potent offensive team. Pittsburgh's lineup included Manny Sanguillen, Willie Stargell, Richie Hebner, and Bob Robertson, who hammered Giants pitching in the 1971 playoffs. Willie McCovey homered twice, the first being career homer No. 400, which made it a truly glorious afternoon for vintage Giants.

San Francisco manager Charlie Fox, who was a bit of a showman, left the dugout to warm up Marichal before the top of the ninth inning. Dave Rader tried to take Marichal's last warmup pitch or two, but Fox elbowed him aside and threw a perfect strike to second base.

September 22, 1973
Giants 5, Padres 2

A crowd—if you can call it that—of 3,148 witnessed Marichal's final victory for the Giants, who unceremoniously sold him to the Red Sox on December 7. Marichal yielded both Padres runs in the first inning; my memory could be faulty but I recall that he was the target of booing. Of course, this thoroughly pissed me off. I wanted to run to the press-box level, grab the public-address microphone from Jeff Carter, and inform the boo-birds that they didn't deserve to watch such a great pitcher. Marichal recovered, allowing five singles in the final eight innings.

Game scores are a fun concept. Devised by the ingenious Bill James, the formula offers a handy way to evaluate the quality of a starting pitcher's performance. Begin with 50 points, add one point for each out recorded (three for each complete inning pitched), add two points for every completed inning after the fourth, and tack on one point for each strikeout. Subtract two points for each hit allowed, four for each run yielded, two for every unearned run scored and one point for each walk. Anything close to 100 for a nine-inning game is excellent.

Intrigued by Madison Bumgarner's blossoming career and his seemingly inevitable climb towards Marichal's level, I decided to look up their top 10 game scores. Mindful of Tim Lincecum's accomplishments, I culled his 10 best game scores, also. This is not an attempt to compare Marichal, Bumgarner, or Lincecum with each other. I'd take any one of them as my starting pitcher. Mainly I wanted to review how marvelous they've been. Here goes:

Marichal

Score	Date	Opp.	IP	H	R	ER	BB	SO
112	7/2/63	MIL	16	8	0	0	4	10
109	5/26/66	PHI	14	6	0	0	1	10
104	8/14/69	NYM	13.1	6	1	1	1	13
96	7/19/60	PHI	9	1	0	0	1	12
94	8/21/61	LAD	9	1	0	0	2	11
91	9/12/63	NYM	9	4	0	0	1	13
90	6/15/63	HOU	9	0	0	0	2	5
90	9/12/69	CIN	9	1	0	0	1	6
88	9/2/64	NYM	9	4	0	0	0	9
88	8/10/71	MTL	9	2	0	0	3	8

Bumgarner

Score	Date	Opp.	IP	H	R	ER	BB	SO
98	7/10/16	ARI	9	1	0	0	1	14
98	8/26/14	COL	9	1	0	0	0	13
94	8/16/15	WAS	9	3	0	0	1	14
94	9/12/15	SD	9	1	0	0	0	9
92	8/3/14	NYM	9	2	0	0	1	10
91	7/28/12	CIN	9	1	0	0	2	8
88*	10/1/14	PIT	9	4	0	0	1	10
87*	10/26/14	KC	9	4	0	0	0	8
87	7/6/10	MIL	8	3	0	0	3	5
85	8/11/15	HOU	9	5	1	1	0	12
85	9/19/16	LAD	7	1	0	0	0	10

Lincecum

Score	Date	Opp.	IP	H	R	ER	BB	SO
96*	10/7/10	ATL	9	2	0	0	1	14
96	7/13/13	SD	9	0	0	0	4	13
92	6/25/14	SD	9	0	0	0	1	6
91	6/29/09	STL	9	2	0	0	0	8
88	9/13/08	SD	9	4	0	0	3	12
87	7/27/09	PIT	9	4	2	0	3	15
87	5/21/11	OAK	9	3	0	0	0	6
87	8/8/13	MIL	8	1	0	0	1	8
85	4/18/09	ARI	8	5	0	0	0	13
83	7/1/07	ARI	7	3	0	0	0	12
83	9/24/10	COL	8	2	1	1	0	9

*Postseason

CHAPTER 9
2014

W e now know that Madison Bumgarner joined the pantheon of postseason icons in 2014. Few people remember that he almost denied himself admission to this exclusive group of performers.

Bumgarner's entry into Game 7 of the 2014 World Series at Kansas City was one of the most dramatic moments during the Giants' stretch of three World Series appearances in five seasons. But the drama briefly appeared headed for disaster.

Summoned before the start of the fifth inning to protect a 3–2 lead, Bumgarner yielded a solid single to the first batter he faced, Omar Infante. "I saw him throw his first couple of pitches, and he looked tired," said Travis Ishikawa, San Francisco's National League Championship Series hero, of Bumgarner. "It was like, 'Oh, no. He's mortal. This isn't good. He's not Bum right now.' The ball looked flat out of his hand. He was missing 'up.'"

Bumgarner *should* have been fatigued. Entering Game 7, he already had pitched 47⅔ postseason innings, just two outs short of matching the record that Arizona's Curt Schilling set in 2001. Bumgarner's total featured 16 innings spanning two victories in the Series over the Royals, including a one-run, three-hit, seven-inning effort in Game 1 and a four-hit shutout in Game 5. Bumgarner would have been the star of the Series even if he hadn't appeared in Game 7.

Giants players sensed that manager Bruce Bochy would call upon Bumgarner sometime during Game 7, though everyone's fondest hope was for starter Tim Hudson, bound for retirement, to deliver a strong final effort, perhaps seven, six, or even five low-scoring innings. Nobody expected Bumgarner, for all his power and durability, to assume the majority of the load.

Said Ishikawa, "When he got through the seventh, I thought, 'Okay, he just gave us three great innings. We've got (Sergio) Romo for the eighth and Cassy (Santiago Casilla) for the ninth.'"

But Bumgarner was bent on finishing the job. Working on two days' rest, he tapped a reserve of energy and retired 14 consecutive batters. The left-hander walked none and struck out four, denying the Royals even the barest shred of hope.

Then, with the Giants one out away from victory, Alex Gordon lined a 1–0 pitch toward left-center field and Gregor Blanco, one of San Francisco's most reliable defenders. Blanco, who preserved Matt Cain's perfect game against Houston in 2012 with a running catch in deep right-center field, charged this ball too aggressively, enabling it to skip past him. As the ball rolled to the base of the wall, where left fielder Juan Perez also misplayed it before finally relaying it to shortstop Brandon Crawford, Gordon raced to third base. The Kauffman Stadium crowd shrieked in happy disbelief.

Fortunately for the Giants, the coolest person at the ballpark held the baseball—the "big donkey," as right-hander Ryan Vogelsong called Bumgarner.

Jeremy Affeldt said of Bumgarner, "He doesn't let anything get too big for him. Something about him enables him to stay super-calm. He never looks at this game as something too much for him to handle. That's what makes him Madison."

The donkey confronted a plowhorse in the form of Salvador Perez, Kansas City's hardworking catcher. The count went to 2–2. Perez fouled off a pitch, then lifted a foul pop-up that stayed in play for third baseman Pablo Sandoval. "Let's go Royals!" the proud Kansas City fans chanted, but their defiance was rendered hollow by the Giants' celebration.

"That was probably the most trying of all our World Series triumphs," Romo said. "Everybody overcame something. Everybody had some kind of issue. Everybody had some kind of stay-cool-I-need-to-man-up kind of moment."

Examples of what Romo meant abounded.

The Giants became the first road team to win Game 7 of a World Series since Pittsburgh defeated Baltimore in 1979. That broke a nine-game losing streak for visiting clubs facing Game 7 in the Series.

San Francisco overcame a 26–41 regular season skid that lasted from June 9 through August 25. That included a 7–22 mark at home from June 9 to August 12.

The Giants hit 69 home runs after June 1, tied for the third-fewest in the majors.

Hudson finished 2–11 in his last 18 starts after bolting to a 7–2 start. Tim Lincecum posted a 4.74 ERA, second-highest of his career, and made just one postseason appearance. The switch-hitting Sandoval batted .199 against left-handers.

Injuries struck hard. Second baseman Marco Scutaro (lower back strain) missed virtually the entire season. Right-hander Matt Cain missed a total of 97 games during three stints on the disabled list and underwent season-ending elbow surgery. Belt missed 96 games with a broken left thumb and a concussion. Center fielder Angel Pagan (back) missed 57 games and needed season-ending surgery September 25 to repair a bulging disc. A left oblique strain shelved outfielder Michael Morse for 24 games in September. And a concussion sidelined catcher Hector Sanchez for 58 games.

* * *

Statistics don't quite capture the scope of Bumgarner's postseason achievements in 2014. But they come close. He never experienced even a mediocre performance while posting a 4–1 record in seven appearances. Even in his lone loss, a 4–1 setback against Washington in Game 3 of the Division Series, he allowed three runs (two earned) on six hits in seven innings. His own throwing error hastened his downfall that night. Bumgarner was nothing less than dominant overall, yielding 28 hits in his record 52⅔ innings as opponents batted .153 off him. He struck out 45 and walked six, maintaining impeccable control even under the postseason's pressurized conditions.

"That postseason was the best my delivery has felt," said Bumgarner, who's not given to extremes or superlatives. "My mechanics were as good as they've ever been, and when everything's going good for you like that—your body feels good, your delivery feels good—your confidence is as high as it can be. And it doesn't hurt that you're in the World Series. That's pretty good for a guy's confidence, too."

Bumgarner pitched two complete games and became the first pitcher in postseason history to record a five-inning save. He appealed to baseball purists who believe that pitchers should finish what they start. These dinosaurs would be thrilled to know that Bumgarner feels the same way, that he'd revel in an era of complete games and pitchers throwing inside without being malicious about it. "I would have loved to have played in the '60s, '70s, and '80s. That's more my speed," he said. "I like the way the game is played now, and the game is definitely progressing with tremendous talent. But I like the mindset of those guys (from the previous generation) a whole lot better."

Hall of Famer Gaylord Perry, a top performer in that period and a fellow North Carolinian, recognized Bumgarner's old-school tendencies. "I see many, many years of great things for him," said Perry, who spent his first 10 seasons in the majors (1962–71) with the Giants. "He has no fear. That's what we love about him."

Perry made that remark after the 2010 World Series.

Bumgarner's ability to physically handle the postseason load suggests that he would have thrived in hardier times for pitchers. He threw 702 pitches in the 2014 postseason, yet returned in 2015 to finish a career-best 18-9. His 2.93 ERA in '15 was his second-lowest for a full season. He increased his strikeouts from 219 to 234 and decreased his walks from 43 to 39.

Barry Zito attributed Bumgarner's steady excellence to his mental approach as much as any physical factors. "He doesn't buy into the attention and the hype," Zito said. "I think there's a beauty in a lot of these guys who are from smaller towns and raised right and raised while kind of keeping things in perspective, to a certain extent, about life. At the end of the day, Bumgarner knows who he is and he doesn't let other people affect that. That lends itself to getting it done on the field in high-pressure situations."

Bumgarner's occasional confrontations with opponents and umpires reflect his inner fire and have become part of who he is on the mound.

"You learn from experience," he said. "Early in my career I would get openly upset, but it's nothing more than my competitive drive. I love competing, and I love nothing more than winning. I compete at everything, not just baseball, throughout the day with family, friends, and teammates. Whatever I'm doing, I'm competing and trying to win. Everybody manages their intensity differently. Some people have that fire that they visibly show, and some people have it but keep it hidden. I try to be aware of my thoughts and feelings, but I don't mind letting out my emotions. Mentally, you still feel the same whether you show it on the field or hold it in.

"Early in my career I would let my thoughts and feelings carry past the moment. It would stay with me the next inning or next couple of innings, and I'd be mentally stuck two or three innings ago. The next thing you know, the game's out of hand, it's a lopsided score and you don't know what happened. For me, the more time you spend trying to hold in your emotions, the tougher it makes it. It's easier to be aware of your emotions, let them go, and move on. You have to be conscious of the situation and move on to the next thing."

The entire 2014 postseason was a triumph for left-hander Madison Bumgarner, who excelled from the Wild Card victory at Pittsburgh to the World Series finale at Kansas City.

* * *

The first thing for the Giants in the postseason was the wild-card game at Pittsburgh. The Pirates' home-field advantage seemed almost oppressive as fans clad in black, one of Pittsburgh's team colors, filled PNC Park. The crowd's enthusiasm, underscored by the "blackout," created an atmosphere of inevitability that portended a Pirates triumph. The observations of a Giants scout who had followed the Pirates for a couple of weeks only accented the feeling that this would be a night to celebrate for Pittsburgh.

"This is a solid defensive team," the scout said, regarding the Pirates admiringly as they took batting practice. "The outfielders throw just as well as their infielders. They've got a balanced lineup with pop, and their bullpen has been really strong."

Meanwhile, Bumgarner had formed his own scouting report. And though it might have been respectful, it was anything but fear-based. Nor did it include plans for bullpen management.

"I remember lacing up my cleats," Affeldt said, "and he's locker partner next to me and he's sitting in his chair and he looks at me and says, 'What do you think you're doing?' I'm like, 'I'm tying my shoes. I'm getting ready to go to the bullpen.' He said, 'You might as well put your tennis shoes on. You ain't pitching this game.' And I looked at him and said, 'What?' And he said, 'You heard me.' And he gets up and walks out. I laughed because I know Bum and I think he's dead serious."

Serious as in a four-hit shutout with one walk and 10 strikeouts. Serious as in three Pirates reaching scoring position. Serious as in an 8–0 decision that thoroughly subdued Pittsburgh—the city as well as the team.

"From pitch one, that guy gave no indication that anybody was going to pitch that game but him," Affeldt marveled. "What a performance!

He has that inside of him mentally; he has that inside of him physically; he has that inside of his heart. When he decides to do something, he's athletically able to do it. After the game, he grabbed me and looked me and said, 'I told you.' "

Given Bumgarner's effectiveness, one run would have sufficed. But he received more when Crawford connected for a fourth-inning grand slam off Pirates starter Edinson Volquez. Though the date was October 1, Crawford's big hit prolonged the success he sustained in September, when he hit a robust .365 with 16 RBIs in 23 games.

"I felt like Craw always had the offensive ability in him," Vogelsong said. "When Craw just does what he's supposed to do in an at-bat, he's an extremely tough out. I think what gets Craw in trouble sometimes is trying to hit the ball over the fence. I get it. Everybody loves home runs and you want to drive your runs in. But to me, Craw is an extremely great hitter when he just plays his game and hits the ball the other way and moves guys over and does all the little things that don't always stand out. I feel like that's what makes him great in the postseason because he just does that stuff, and if he runs into one he runs into one."

Each of the nine games in the next two postseason series was decided by three runs or less. Obviously, a lot of solid, taut baseball unfolded. Yet each series will be remembered mostly for one game. The focal point of the Division Series against Washington was Game 2, the 2–1, 18-inning affair featuring Yusmeiro Petit's six shutout innings of relief and Brandon Belt's tiebreaking homer in the 18th. The National League Championship Series against St. Louis will live forever in television replays, represented by Ishikawa's three-run, walk-off homer that won Game 5 for the Giants 6–3 and sent them to the World Series.

Petit rarely had much to say. Had he been more loquacious, he might have asked Bochy, "Why don't I pitch more?" His role as long reliever and spot starter doomed him to infrequent appearances. As hyperactive bullpens proliferated throughout baseball, Petit appeared in only 39 games in 2014. And though he made 12 starts, he amassed only 117 innings. So it was a well-rested Petit who reported for duty in the 12th inning of Game 2.

Petit walked the first batter he faced, an ominous sign for a pitcher who never went to a three-ball count while facing a stretch of 70 consecutive batters from September 2 through 20, 2014. He recovered quickly against Washington, retiring 13 of the final 14 batters he faced while striking out the side in the 14th inning. He ultimately surrendered one hit and walked three.

Facing Tanner Roark, Belt led off the 18th for the Giants, which was newsworthy enough. San Francisco's first baseman weathered three stints on the disabled list, once with a broken left thumb and twice due to a concussion. He connected with a full-count pitch that made him only the third Giant to hit an extra-inning homer in postseason history. Hall of Famer Mel Ott (1933) and 1954 World Series hero Dusty Rhodes were the others.

The game's duration—a whopping six hours and 23 minutes, about as long as a coast-to-coast flight—forced most writers to stay in the press box after the game to write and thus compensate as much as they could for unavoidably blown deadlines. One writer was free to head for the interview room and quiz Belt about his heroics. Yes, you guessed him. I blurted questions concerning the difficulty of staying focused through such a long game, how he felt emotionally while rounding the bases, his perspective on Petit's performance, and about the team's mindset with a 2–0 lead in the best-of-five series. As Steve Martin said during his days as a standup comic, "The most amazing thing to me is, I get paid for doing this."

Belt admitted that staying focused was indeed challenging, accounting for his 0-for-6 performance at the plate before he homered. "It was tough at times," he said. "That was something I had to kind of figure out before the last at-bat. I knew I wasn't having great at-bats the entire game. I wasn't sticking with the plan that I had in the previous five or six games. I had to restart a little bit. Just get a good at-bat, and whatever happens, happens. I just wanted to get on base for the guys behind me. 'Get 'em on, get 'em over, and get 'em in.' Fortunately, I put a good enough swing on it." Running out the homer, Belt said, was "something you dream about your entire life. I am very fortunate I was able to experience it." He described Petit as "amazing" and "awesome," then concluded predictably by insisting that the Giants would not take Washington for granted.

Jump to Game 5 of the NLCS, which began with the Giants leading the series 3–1. During the postseason, San Francisco's lineup had remained a curiosity. The Giants lacked a true left fielder, since Michael Morse, who played a team-high 84 games at that spot during the regular season, was bothered by a strained oblique muscle. Gregor Blanco was needed in center field. So Bochy, unafraid of trying something different, started Ishikawa in left field for 14 of San Francisco's 17 postseason games. Bochy correctly figured that Ishikawa, a first baseman by trade, was athletic enough to handle the position. Besides, to echo what Vogelsong said of Crawford, Ishikawa might run into one.

At 31, Ishikawa had ceased to be a prospect.

After spending 2009–10 with the Giants, he migrated through five organizations from 2011 through 2013. He re-signed with the Giants, the team with which he was the most familiar, in late April of 2014. But, believing that only an unusual combination of circumstances would allow him to return to the majors, a despondent Ishikawa contemplated retiring. It was at about this time that the Giants purchased his contract on July 29, needing depth behind the injury-prone Belt and Morse.

Ishikawa's potential to be a defensive liability finally occurred in the third inning against the Cardinals when he played Jon Jay's fly ball into an RBI double. That opened the scoring, and by the eighth inning St. Louis still led 3–2. Morse, limited to pinch-hitting, batted for Bumgarner and christened the Giants' half of the inning with a home run off Pat Neshek to pull the Giants even. St. Louis loaded the bases with two outs in the ninth, but Affeldt relieved Casilla and ended the threat.

That's how Ishikawa came to be facing Michael Wacha with two on, one out, and the score still tied in the ninth inning. Ishikawa connected with a 2–0 pitch and entrenched himself in Giants postseason history in the few seconds it took for the ball to reach AT&T Park's right-field arcade.

Nearly two years later, Ishikawa still spoke with wonder about the kaleidoscope of events that swirled around the Giants.

"There were just so many cool stories from that season," Ishikawa said. "Just look at every postseason series we had—Craw with the grand slam and Bum with the shutout, and you think of Petit and Belt in the Washington series and even [Jake] Peavy in the first game [of the Division Series], going against their ace [Stephen Strasburg] and giving us that opportunity to get that win.

"And you think of Mikey-Mo with the big eighth inning. I love my home run, but I lost my voice on his home run. Because I had that big error, that big misplay in the outfield. So to tie that game in that situation off a nasty right-handed sidearm guy [Neshek] and Mikey doing that—that was so uplifting that you almost had to feel like we were going to win the game when he did that. And then obviously Affeldt coming in with the bases loaded in the ninth and getting the ground-out to lead to that. There were so many things that could have led to me not being in that situation had it not been for those guys around me."

One of those guys happened to be the manager. Ishikawa figuratively tipped his cap to Bochy and cited himself as a pawn whom the manager used so skillfully.

Ishikawa pointed out that Juan Perez, a legitimate defensive out-fielder, replaced him during postseason games when the Giants led or were tied in the late innings. One occasion when he didn't do this was Game 5 of the NLCS. That occasion ended with Ishikawa sprinting around the bases and being mobbed by teammates at home plate.

"I think he's got an intuition or a gut feeling that goes against what prototypical baseball says," Ishikawa said. "There were moves he would make that on paper don't make sense. But they always seem to work out."

Had Bochy stuck with his postseason pattern, Ishikawa would have started Game 7 of the World Series, since a right-hander—Jeremy Guthrie—was starting for Kansas City. Instead, Perez got the start in left field. As Ishikawa related, Bochy told him, "We want to go with defense here. It's nothing against you, it's just that obviously Juan's a better outfielder." Replied Ishikawa, "I want to win this World Series. So if you feel like that's going to help, I'm all for it."

Handling the designated hitter's role to perfection, Morse drove in runs with a second-inning sacrifice fly and a fourth-inning single to help the Giants assume a 3–2 advantage that ultimately would be the final score. With one out in the fifth inning and Omar Infante on second base, Perez contributed a running catch on Nori Aoki's line drive. Perez made the play look simple by getting a good jump on the ball. He crossed into foul territory several feet after making the catch, reflecting how closely the drive paralleled the foul line. Would Ishikawa have snared Aoki's liner, or might it have eluded him for an RBI double? Said Ishikawa, "I want to say I can make that catch, but I don't think there's a better guy out there than Juan Perez. Even if he didn't get a hit that game, that might have saved the Series. Because he was there to make that play. I don't know if I was quick enough to get to that ball."

Bochy, concluded Ishikawa, "definitely has a sixth sense. And he listens to it."

CHAPTER 10
NO-HITTERS

I was doing just fine as I wrote my main story on Matt Cain's perfect game. My adrenaline was pumping, my mind was racing—I was in my little cocoon of postgame intensity, free from distractions.

Then a little factoid flew into my skull as if it were a foul ball hit into the press box. Cain had just thrown the 22nd perfect game in major league history. That meant America, our great country, has had more presidents than perfect games. What we had witnessed that night at AT&T Park was rarer than the next person to adjust his or her desk chair in the Oval Office.

Then I got a little emotional. But I didn't let anybody notice.

I'm a fortunate individual for numerous reasons. From a baseball perspective, I'm virtually certain that seeing seven no-hitters puts me in the 99th percentile of that category. I've met people who've seen more baseball than me yet haven't witnessed a single no-no. And to think that, with a little more luck, my no-hitter count could be in double figures. I saw Yusmeiro Petit and Matt Moore lose their no-hit bids with one out to go (Petit was one *strike* away from a perfect game), and I was staying home to cover the draft when Chris Heston threw his 2015 no-hitter at New York.

Then again, I believe that the baseball gods exist, and thus I'm sure they were at work when a logistical mixup prevented me from covering the 2013 All-Star Game. Had everything gone as originally planned, I would have been in New York on July 13, 2013, when Tim Lincecum threw his first no-hitter. So I'll never complain about what I've missed.

If you've never seen a no-hitter in person, I hope you do someday. Here's a sampling of what you have to look forward to:

Ed Halicki, Giants
August 24, 1975
6–0 over Mets

This was the second game of a doubleheader. I was thoroughly entertained in the first game when Dave Kingman hit a grand slam off Jim Barr. Kingman began his career with the Giants, who never could figure out where to play him. Let's just say that I thought he released a little frustration when he stepped on home plate ("stomped" is more like it) after rounding the bases.

Then Kingman got blown away like all the rest of the Mets when Halicki took over. Every Mets starter except John Milner struck out at least once; Kingman and Rusty Staub each struck out twice. I think I pretty much yelled nonstop from the seventh inning on.

I distinctly recall pinch-hitter Jesus Alou, rotating his head and all, fouling out to open the ninth, and I remember Wayne Garrett grounding out to end the game. I kept the next day's newspapers, and what struck me was how close Halicki came to *not* pitching a no-hitter. Steve Ontiveros, replacing injured right fielder Bobby Murcer, dove to snare Felix Millan's sinking liner in the first inning. Staub hit a fifth-inning smash that might have proceeded into center field had it not caromed off Halicki's leg to second baseman Derrel Thomas, who fumbled it for an error.

It was the first and only no-hitter thrown at Candlestick Park during the 1970–78 phase when artificial turf covered the playing surface.

Jerry Reuss
June 27, 1980
8–0 over Giants

This game taught me that a pitcher doesn't need to look like he has no-hit stuff to have no-hit stuff. Reuss didn't appear overpowering—he struck out only two batters!—but the Giants posed no threat. It definitely wasn't a typical Giants–Dodgers affair. Jack Clark reached safely on a Bill Russell error in the first inning. Otherwise, Reuss could have had a perfect game.

Odd things would tend to happen at Candlestick Park when it was actually hot there, and this was an unusually steamy night. The down jackets and sweaters stayed in the car.

I watched part of the game from the Stadium Club as a guest of a college buddy. It was the only time I ever set foot inside the place. I didn't keep score, but I have a Stadium Club matchbook lying around somewhere.

Jonathan Sanchez
July 10, 2009
8–0 over Padres

I have this bad habit of showing up sat the ballpark on off-days. Occasionally I do so out of sheer stupidity because I read the schedule incorrectly. Sometimes I simply can't find anything better to do. In this case, it was the latter.

The Black Eyed Peas' "I Gotta Feelin'" blared over the public-address system at AT&T Park when Sanchez strode to the mound to warm up before the seventh or eighth inning. You know—"I got a feeling that tonight's gonna be a good night...." Nobody thinks that the game's final pitch to Everth Cabrera was a strike, but who cares?

Sanchez always had fabulous stuff but incomplete understanding of how to use it. He drove pitching coach Dave Righetti and bullpen coach Mark Gardner nuts. In fact, Sanchez relieved in his two appearances immediately preceding the no-hitter in an attempt to correct some flaws.

Remarkably, Sanchez walked nobody. Of course, you know what's next: Juan Uribe, having moved to third base from second, misplayed Chase Headley's eighth-inning grounder for an error to deny Sanchez a chance at a perfect game.

Matt Cain
June 13, 2012
10–0 over Astros

On this night, there would be no, "He would have had a perfect game if only...." This was the real thing.

And Cain deserved it. He had pitched in tough luck during his first few big league seasons, receiving poor run support. In 2008, when he finished 8–14, his run support was the National League's worst. Future Dodgers manager Dave Roberts, who was finishing his playing career as a Giants outfielder, counseled Cain about maintaining his confidence. Cain was hardly fragile emotionally, but even the toughest of performers can crumble when they repeatedly receive no breaks.

Cain had nothing to worry about. The Giants scored in each of the first five innings, so the game's outcome was not an issue. Right fielder Gregor Blanco made the evening's signature defensive play when he christened the seventh inning by racing into the right-center gap to haul in Jordan Schafer's long drive.

Speaking of long drives, witnesses should have sensed hours before the game that something special was in store for Cain. Golf's U.S. Open was set to begin the next day at San Francisco's Olympic Club, and it just so happened that a handful of pros showed up at AT&T Park for a photo opportunity just as the Giants began batting practice (some golfers stayed for the game). Typically, starting pitchers refrain from doing anything before a game that could be remotely construed as goofing off. But an unconcerned Cain grabbed a driver, teed up a ball, and hit it about nine miles into San Francisco Bay.

Matt Cain acknowledges the appreciative AT&T Park crowd after fashioning his perfect game against the Houston Astros. Standing behind Cain, Giants mascot Lou Seal displays a hastily scrawled yet appropriate sign.

Cain's 14 strikeouts were a personal best and tied Sandy Koufax's 1965 record for most strikeouts in a perfect game. Cain went to six three-ball counts but survived, throwing 86 strikes in 125 pitches. He recorded the final out on Jason Castro's weak grounder to third baseman Joaquin Arias, who made a strong throw to first base. Arias, who underwent shoulder surgery in 2007, later admitted that he probably wouldn't have been able to make the same throw in time a year or two earlier.

Homer Bailey
July 2, 2013
3–0 over Giants

The Giants didn't get ambushed at Cincinnati's Great American Ball Park. They knew good and well how dominant Bailey could be. In Game 3 of the previous year's Division Series, the right-hander limited San Francisco to one hit in seven innings. The Giants mustered a run off him, but it was without benefit of a hit.

Bailey appeared mortal only in the seventh inning, when he walked Blanco on a full-count pitch. After Marco Scutaro's weak grounder advanced Blanco to second base, Bailey broke late from the mound on Buster Posey's grounder to first baseman Joey Votto. Realizing that he might not have a play on Posey, Votto threw to third to retire Blanco and preserve the no-hitter.

Bailey became the first pitcher since Nolan Ryan (1974–75) to throw the final no-hitter of one season and the first no-hitter of the next. He silenced Pittsburgh on September 28, 2012.

Tim Lincecum
July 13, 2013
9–0 over Padres

This was Lincecum's 25th career appearance against San Diego. He had allowed two or fewer earned runs in 15 of the previous 24. In fact, Lincecum no-hit the Padres for six innings the night before Sanchez pitched his no-hitter. But that Lincecum was in the middle of his second consecutive Cy Young Award–winning season. This Lincecum owned a 4–9 record with a 4.61 ERA. However, he remained capable of dazzling hitters. In his previous start, he struck out 11 Mets in seven innings while allowing three runs and seven hits in a no-decision.

On this night at Petco Park, Lincecum was just a little rough around the edges. He issued a first-inning walk and hit a batter in the second. Then he recorded six consecutive swinging strikeouts, a clear sign that he was on the brink of sustaining a remarkable effort.

Lincecum's pitch count, however, was rising quickly. He lived particularly dangerously in the sixth inning, sandwiching a pair of strikeouts around a walk to Cabrera. Lincecum walked Headley after Cabrera stole second base and advanced to third on a wild pitch. But Carlos Quentin lined out to shortstop, ending the threat.

San Francisco's defense helped Lincecum in the late innings. Third baseman Pablo Sandoval made a slick play on pinch-hitter Jesus Guzman's grounder to end the seventh. Right fielder Hunter Pence made a spectacular catch on Alexi Amarista's sinking liner to conclude the eighth.

Lincecum entered the ninth inning having thrown 138 pitches, but manager Bruce Bochy had no intention of removing him. "He wouldn't have talked to me the rest of the year if I had taken him out," Bochy said. Lincecum coaxed 29 swings and misses, his all-time regular season high.

Tim Lincecum

June 25, 2014

4–0 over Padres

In relative terms, this one was drama-free. No defensive gymnastics were necessary, though the Padres hit a few balls hard. Lincecum wasn't overly electrifying, but was definitely efficient, issuing one walk while striking out six.

The Giants (11) actually struck out more than the Padres (six). But Lincecum, of all people, partially compensated by singling twice and scoring twice. Posey led the offense by going 4-for-4 with two RBIs.

Posey played first base, enabling Hector Sanchez to be part of a milestone.

Once again, this game found Lincecum in a mini slump. He entered the afternoon 5–5 with a 4.90 ERA.

CHAPTER 11
THE NICEST MAN

I anticipated a response to my interview request. I had no idea I'd receive a laugh and a lasting memory with it. "Is this *the* Chris Haft?" said Willie McCovey, in a playful tone.

I must confess that being gently teased by a Hall of Famer and San Francisco icon dissolved any professional detachment I might have felt. This was not my first telephone conversation with McCovey, but it was by far the best. If an armored truck filled with cash had arrived at my residence at that moment, I would have told the driver to leave, because I already felt like a million bucks. Five words from McCovey was all it took.

Willie Lee McCovey shall forever be known as a power hitter. In his case, this gift extends beyond the batter's box and his career total of 521 homers. McCovey always possessed the power to warm people's hearts, and he retained it long after his final at-bat on July 6, 1980. Maybe he'd do this with a few words, as was the case with me. Often, his presence or simply his expression would suffice.

"If he walked into a room and smiled, everybody in that room smiled," said catcher Hobie Landrith, a member of the Giants when McCovey broke into the majors in 1959. "When you can create that kind of an environment, you're a special person."

"He has that poker face," former Giants executive Pat Gallagher said, "but he also has that great smile."

Giants president Larry Baer described McCovey as "really thoughtful, really sensitive, really caring." McCovey demonstrated these qualities in 1978 as he approached hitting his 500th career home run. Through Puma, the shoe company who manufactured the cleats McCovey wore, he ordered T-shirts commemorating his milestone homer. To personalize the gesture, McCovey had each player's nickname printed on the shirt he received. So third baseman Darrell Evans got the one reserved for "Doody." "Ho-ho" went to right-hander Ed Halicki. Of course, "The

Count" was for John Montefusco. And so on. After distributing the shirts, Giants batboy Patrick Quinlan reported to McCovey emptyhanded. Or so Quinlan thought. Handing Quinlan a shirt with his first name on it, McCovey said, "Did you think I forgot you, Pat?"

During an offseason luncheon at the Double Play, a tavern neighboring the site of Seals Stadium, the Giants' first San Francisco home, Baer reminisced about sitting on McCovey's lap at age five or six during a promotional appearance by the slugging first baseman at a Home Savings & Loan branch on Geary Street. When McCovey received his turn to speak, he opened with, "I think my knee problems began that day Larry sat on them." The room exploded with laughter.

McCovey didn't mind sharing his identity, so to speak. He was nicknamed "Stretch," owing to his ability to extend his 6'4" frame impossibly far for throws. Naturally, hundreds of Bay Area residents with above-average height and flexibility acquired the same moniker due to McCovey's popularity. One of them was 5'10" Julie Pilossoph, a third-generation San Franciscan who played first base for the "Straight Shots," a city women's softball league team. Through intermediaries, Pilossoph received an autographed photo from the real "Stretch," who inscribed the 8-by-10 glossy, "To Stretch—Best Wishes."

The Bay Area embraced McCovey, and he reciprocated. When the 49ers played at Kezar Stadium, he casually strolled to their games, mixing easily with the fans. He attended and hosted countless charity functions. Once he even took in Opening Night at the San Francisco Opera, which in that city is the World Series, Super Bowl, and New Year's Eve all rolled into one.

"I always had a connection here in the city from the first day I arrived," McCovey said.

Small wonder. That was quite a day, to say the least. McCovey experienced one of the most prolific debuts in professional sports history, going

4-for-4 off future Hall of Famer Robin Roberts with three runs scored and a pair of RBIs in a 7–2 victory over Philadelphia on July 30, 1959.

"He got four bloop hits off me. Tell Willie I said that," Roberts joked in a 2009 interview. More seriously, Roberts said, "You could tell Willie was going to be a problem for a lot of guys, not just me."

McCovey's .270 lifetime batting average might have seemed pedestrian. But his skills commanded respect, if not sheer awe. From 1965 to 1970, a period dominated by superb starting pitchers, McCovey totaled 226 home runs—an average of 38 per season—matched in the major leagues only by Hank Aaron. McCovey's 636 RBIs during that span (106 per year) led all major leaguers, as did his .405 on-base percentage and .578 slugging percentage. He also batted a respectable .291.

McCovey made the damnedest out I've ever seen, and I don't mean his vicious line drive to Yankees second baseman Bobby Richardson that ended the 1962 World Series and stranded runners in scoring position (McCovey: "I could have hit it in a different direction, that's for sure."). In August 1977, I journeyed south for a Giants–Dodgers series at Los Angeles. Batting in the late innings of the series opener, McCovey lifted a pop fly that Dodgers second baseman Davey Lopes began to pursue. Then it was right fielder Reggie Smith's turn. Smith kept retreating and retreating until he finally snagged the fly with his back against the Dodger Stadium wall. What initially looked like an infield fly darned near turned out to be a home run.

Others were more prolific than McCovey during their careers or certain time frames. Yet if I were compiling an illustrated dictionary of baseball terms, I'd seek a photograph of McCovey, whose career spanned four decades (1959–80), to accompany "cleanup hitter." No less a man than Bob Gibson, probably the most imposing pitcher among all the greats who competed during that interval, called McCovey "the scariest hitter in baseball" in Lonnie Wheeler's *Sixty Feet, Six Inches*. The Giants'

Willie McCovey's smile is infectious, as is proven again during a meeting between the slugger and this book's author. McCovey's enduring popularity among Giants fans has made him a San Francisco icon.

lineup of the early- to mid-1960s was loaded with accomplished hitters, including Willie Mays, Orlando Cepeda, Felipe Alou, and Jim Ray Hart. Nevertheless, Gibson added, "None of the others put the fear in me that McCovey did. Not even Mays."

Intentional walks were an overlooked stratagem until 1969, when McCovey won the National League's Most Valuable Player award. He drew 45 intentional passes that year, which remained a record until Barry Bonds eclipsed it in 2002. The following tale is perhaps apochryphal, but it conveys the terror mingled with admiration that McCovey generated: one day during his sovereignty over all big league sluggers, he received another intentional walk, this one ordered by Cincinnati manager Sparky Anderson. Especially frustrated on this occasion over having the bat figuratively removed from his hands, McCovey peered into the Reds dugout en route to first base and growled at Anderson, "Who do you think I am, Babe Ruth?" Anderson replied, "No. You're better."

Though McCovey never won a Gold Glove award for defensive excellence, the first-ballot Hall of Fame inductee mastered all aspects of playing first base. This was quite challenging at San Francisco's Candlestick Park, where the wind unexpectedly altered the course of pop flies and blow-dried the infield dirt, rendering grounders and short-hop throws treacherous.

"He was a better first baseman than people believed," Giants catcher Jack Hiatt said. "I tell you something else he could do then. He could *fly*. Those big, long legs would touch the ground maybe seven times on the way from first to third."

More often, however, McCovey played through extreme discomfort in his knees.

"You could always tell that he was in pain," outfielder Ken Henderson said.

Echoed Hiatt, "He was in that training room every day. Then he'd go out and give you 150 percent."

McCovey's drive to play trumped all pain. He was a deathly serious competitor, though his intensity went largely unnoticed due to his near-total absence of demonstrative behavior. One thing's certain: The phrase "playing the game right" definitely applied to him.

McCovey took a dim view of unnecessary histrionics, even if a teammate violated that code. Right-hander Jim Barr recalled incurring McCovey's wrath in a 1977 game against San Diego after firing a fastball high and tight to George Hendrick, who liked to extend his arms as he swung and thus received inside pitches steadily. Said Barr, who had superior control, "We knew how to pitch inside to brush a guy back. We knew how to pitch inside to knock a guy down. There was a difference." On this occasion, Barr came a little too close to hitting Hendrick, who never complained about such treatment. "It was right after a couple of things happened on the field, so it kind of looked like I was trying to knock him down," Barr said. "The catcher throws the ball back to me, and as soon as I catch the ball, I look out of the corner of my eye and here comes Mac. He's standing 15 feet from me. He walks up to me and looks me in the eyes and goes, 'What the hell are you doing?' And I went, 'Mac, I didn't try that. I did *not* try that.' He says, 'You better not have,' and walks back to first."

That was the McCovey the Giants saw during his 19 seasons with them—an exceedingly dignified man who commanded unswerving respect and said a lot with a little.

Said Barr, "How can you not (respect him)? Mac wasn't a guy who'd say two words about himself. He never really argued with anybody. He just went out there and did his job hard and did it well."

"He was a great teammate," Hiatt said. "He was very complimentary. 'Nice going, Jack.' Coming from him, that was high praise."

McCovey was such a towering figure that on the rare occasions when he felt he was treated less than fairly, it made news.

On July 18, 1972, Expos reliever John Strohmayer hit McCovey with an 0–2 pitch on the right arm, the same one he broke in San Diego during the season-opening series. As Bob Stevens of the San Francisco *Chronicle* wrote, "For the first time in memory, McCovey became angry on the field. He challenged Strohmayer to everything but a duel with machetes at dawn and several times appeared ready to go after the Expo."

Understand that nobody threw at McCovey, ever. During his prime, which is to say throughout most of his career, Mays was routinely brushed back and knocked down. It was the only recourse for many pitchers, who were overmatched by his immense talent. Other stars routinely encountered similar treatment, most famously Frank Robinson of the Cincinnati Reds whenever he'd face Dodgers right-hander Don Drysdale.

But McCovey? "I never saw Willie Mac go down," Hiatt said. "No. No. You don't go there."

Early in the 1978 season, a dispute between McCovey and club management over who would pay for his hotel suite on the road spilled into the media. "McCovey may quit," read the lead headline in the sports section of the May 12, 1978, San Francisco *Chronicle*. If team officials were hoping that public reaction would force McCovey to back down, they were wrong. The ovations for him at Candlestick Park grew louder. "Maybe McCovey should run for governor," suggested a San Francisco *Examiner* headline on May 14. McCovey got his suite, and the controversy ended.

Nothing stopped Giants fans from cheering for McCovey, not even the October 25, 1973, trade that sent him and outfielder Bernie Williams to the San Diego Padres for left-hander Mike Caldwell. He even hit five home runs in San Francisco while playing for the Padres, helping him accumulate his record total of 231 homers at Candlestick. He rejoined the Giants in 1977, furthering the organization's renaissance, which resulted in a staggering attendance increase from 700,056 that year to 1,740,477 in 1978. Ending a four-year streak of sub-.500 records obviously helped. But McCovey's impact was also beyond question.

"It gave us some credibility," Gallagher said of McCovey's return. "It restored some of the pride in the uniform. He added a certain amount of respect that the organization couldn't really get any other way."

Before the '78 season began, McCovey approached Bill Madlock with a request: Move from third base to second, which would enable Darrell Evans to play third and thus improve the club. Madlock praised

McCovey for being "just unbelievable, with his professionalism and everything. He was a pleasure to be with. When somebody like that, who you know is a Hall of Famer, asks you to do that, how could you turn him down?"

The naming of the Willie Mac Award winner, held annually before the regular season's final Friday night home game, has become one of the most anticipated dates on the club's schedule. The award is given to the season's most inspiring Giant based on a vote among players, coaches, the manager, the athletic training staff, and McCovey himself. Fan balloting accounts for a small percentage of the vote.

Asked Baer rhetorically, "The Willie Mac Award, what's it about? It's about team. It's about who's the most respected teammate. Everybdy respects Willie Mac. In every possible way."

As the Giants' director of marketing and business affairs in 1980, Gallagher developed the idea for the Willie Mac Award. The 49ers set a precedent with their Len Eshmont Award, which is also bestowed upon an especially inspiring performer. The only problem with it was that relatively few fans knew that Eshmont was a running back and defensive back who played on the original 1946 49ers squad and scored the first touchdown in team history. "Obviously he was somebody who commanded a lot of respect," Gallagher said. "But McCovey was different. He was unassailable, the way he carried himself and did everything."

Giants players fully grasp the Willie Mac Award's significance. "First of all, it's an amazing honor, because it's voted on by your teammates and the coaches," 2011 winner Ryan Vogelsong said. "I know the fans have a little bit of a vote, but the highest percentage comes from the guys you're with every day. Any time that you get recognized by the guys you play with every night, that means a lot."

"It's something that is so much bigger than the game of baseball," 1989 winner Dave Dravecky said.

Cherishing the award's link to McCovey, Pence added, "To have your name mentioned with his, it's an honor."

"He's always such a class guy," 2001 winner Mark Gardner said. "He'll talk to you any time. He was such a great player. A lot of great players don't have the time of day for you. And he always does."

The Willie Mac Award guarantees that McCovey will remain synonymous with greatness as long as the franchise exists. The same goes for the naming of McCovey Cove, the portion of San Francisco Bay beyond the right-field stands where dozens, perhaps hundreds, of his home runs would land if he were playing today. Moreover, the scope of McCovey's career and the style he displayed are easy to recall and impossible to duplicate.

"He's a man of integrity, he's a man of character, and he's a Giant," Dravecky said.

AFTERWORD

The Giants didn't forget how to win in 2016. When to win, however, became a critical issue.

San Francisco built its streak of World Series triumphs in even-numbered years with a simple recipe: combine two reliable starters with a pinch of a third, add one effective closer, and mix for four to seven games.

In 2010, this worked with Tim Lincecum, Matt Cain, Madison Bumgarner, and Brian Wilson.

They again heeded directions in 2012, using Cain, Ryan Vogelsong, and Barry Zito before throwing in Sergio Romo.

Then they loosely stuck to the plan in 2014, going heavy on Bumgarner with dashes of Santiago Casilla here and there.

San Francisco cooked too soon in 2016, finishing the first half with the major leagues' best record (57–33) before the bullpen, which lacked a reliable closer, burned out. The Giants reached the postseason, but served up a microcosm of their year in Game 4 of the Division Series against the Cubs by failing to hold a 5–2 lead in the ninth inning. Chicago rallied for four runs to beat the Giants 6–5, and continued its surge until 108 years of World Series futility had ended.

The Indians–Cubs World Series matchup was meaningful for two of the most prominent nonuniformed Giants—broadcast partners Duane Kuiper and Mike Krukow. Both of them readily acknowledged that this was a meaningful series for them.

Kuiper spent his first 10 professional seasons in the Indians organization, including 1974–81 in the majors as a second baseman. None of those teams finished higher than fourth in the powerful American League East.

"The years that I played there, we were hit over the head about the Indians not having been involved in a world championship for 'X' amount of years," Kuiper said.

Krukow pitched for five years (1977–81) with the Cubs. They twice finished last and never placed higher than third in that span. He knew that Cubs fans were ready for their close-up, so to speak, in the 2016 postseason. "They are going to have fun with it, they are going to embrace it, and they are going to enjoy every second as if they're not going to have another one for 108 more years," Krukow said.

The Giants didn't need even 108 seconds to decipher what went wrong in 2016 and how they can improve for 2017. They amassed a major league–high 30 blown saves, a franchise record since saves became an official statistic in 1969. San Francisco also lost a franchise-record nine games in 2016 when leading entering the ninth inning. Five of those defeats occurred in September. Moreover, the Giants lost six regular season games after leading by four runs or more, matching Colorado for the big league lead in this category.

Overall, the Giants' foundation for success—pitching and defense—remained strong, which boded well for the near future. San Francisco's starters ranked fifth in the majors with a 3.71 ERA. The Giants' defensive credentials were just as impressive, as they led all teams with a .988 fielding percentage. If you prefer modern metrics, the Giants ranked third in the majors with 50 defensive runs saved, according to FanGraphs.

Bumgarner continued to build his legend by pitching his second four-hit shutout on the road in the last three wild-card games as the Giants eliminated the Mets 3–0. That extended Bumgarner's postseason streak of scoreless innings to 23, which grew to 24 before the Cubs snapped it in the Division Series. The left-hander's road ERA in the postseason is a microscopic 0.50 (three earned runs in 53⅔ innings spanning eight appearances).

"To Bum, this is just another game," right-hander Jeff Samardzija said. "Everybody knows it's not. Everybody knows it's not easy. But he's so unflappable."

Said reliever George Kontos, "This kind of stamped him as a legend, in my mind."

During the regular season, Bumgarner became the fifth pitcher in franchise history to strike out at least 200 batters in three consecutive seasons. Preceding Bumgarner were Hall of Famers Christy Mathewson, Amos Rusie, and Juan Marichal and the ever-popular Tim Lincecum.

Bumgarner ranked among NL leaders in multiple categories, including strikeouts, ERA, complete games, innings, opponents' batting average, walks and hits per inning pitched, and quality starts. The 27-year-old also struck out at least 10 batters in five games through mid-September, hiking his career total of such performances to 30. Only Lincecum (36) has more in Giants history. Moreover, Bumgarner set a franchise single-season record for left-handed pitchers by striking out 251. Cy Seymour owned the previous mark with 244 in 1898.

Johnny Cueto's reputation hasn't reached Bumgarner's near-mythic proportions yet, but he performed like a magician. Cueto's hocus-pocus, featuring his ability to create a wide variety of pitches, enabled him to post an 18-5 record with a 2.79 ERA. Cueto leaves the impression that he never throws the same pitch twice. He doesn't just throw. He improvises. He might accelerate his delivery to fire a "quick pitch" that disrupts the hitter's timing. Or he'll turn his back in midmotion toward the hitter for an extra beat or two, effectively hiding the ball from his foe. Occasionally in mid-delivery he'll rock his shoulders back and forth in a "shimmy" that's almost guaranteed to confuse a batter.

Samardzija proved durable, working at least five innings in 27 of 30 starts. He indicated that he derived extra motivation by being surrounded by San Francisco's group of talented starting pitchers, particularly Bumgarner and Cueto.

"It's a real competitive staff we have here, man," Samardzija said. "It's real fun to be in the middle of it, watching these guys work in front of me.

You can't really let up when the guys in front of you are going seven, eight, nine innings. You have to show up every day and keep pace."

Trade Deadline acquisition Matt Moore was the No. 4 starter in terms of sequence only. Down the stretch he performed as if he ranked much higher on San Francisco's pecking order, winning six of his last eight starts. Moore's season ended in bittersweet fashion, as he sustained an impressive performance in Game 4 of the Division Series—an eight-inning two-hitter in which he struck out 10 and allowed two runs (one earned). But, wary of physically taxing Moore, who had thrown 120 pitches, manager Bruce Bochy turned the game over to the bullpen, and you know what happened after that.

Sounding ready to bounce back with the rest of the team, Moore said, "It's a tough one to end on, for sure, but, at least from what I can see, it definitely seems like there are a lot of guys who are very confident and understand who they are."

That would describe catcher Buster Posey, shortstop Brandon Crawford, and second baseman Joe Panik, who led the Giants' competent defense by winning Gold Glove awards. The Giants had not boasted that many recipients of the award since 1993, when left fielder Barry Bonds, catcher Kirt Manwaring, second baseman Robby Thompson, and third baseman Matt Williams were recipients.

The awards reflected each Giant's lifelong attention to defense, as well as the club's ongoing emphasis on that facet of the game.

Posey said that defense was a "bigger focal point" with his coaches and father when he was a youth. Switching from shortstop to catcher at Florida State University only intensified the need for Posey to concentrate on defense.

Posey's stature is beyond question. Many experts consider him a legitimate Hall of Fame candidate. Despite his relatively quiet facade, he has become a leader by example on the field and in the clubhouse.

"Like anything, there's a balance and a fine line," Posey said. "I want to help, but I think for somebody to maximize their potential, they have to figure things out on their own."

Crawford, a Gold Glove recipient for the second year in a row, reiterated that he always enjoyed taking ground balls as a youth. "It wasn't really punishment for me," Crawford said. Thus, he said that the Gold Glove "will always be special to me."

Crawford added that the team places a "high priority" on defense. "We all feed off of each other," he said.

Like most Gold Glove winners, Crawford can also excel at the plate. He rapped seven hits in a 14-inning standoff at Miami on August 8, which he settled with an RBI single to provide an 8–7 victory for the Giants. The soft-spoken Crawford admitted knowing that his hit total was lengthening along with the game. "I don't care how long the game is," Crawford said. "Everybody knows how many hits they have in a game."

Panik recalled that his father would make him refine his defensive skills before allowing him to hit during family trips to the local park.

Crawford called Panik "well-rounded" and said that he has especially improved at turning double plays. "You look at him, there's not too many weaknesses."

Panik unseated Colorado's DJ LeMahieu, the 2015 winner, despite playing only 127 games due to a concussion that sidelined him in June.

Nevertheless, said Panik, "I don't want to say I was surprised."

Panik endured back problems in 2015 but reclaimed his position. He demonstrated his steadiness by ranking as the majors' toughest player to strike out for much of the season (once every 11.2 at-bats). Panik compensated for his slumping teammates by thriving in August, when he batted .276 and compiled an .862 OPS (on-base plus slugging percentage).

Limited to 52 games in 2015 while coping with wrist, forearm, and oblique injuries, Hunter Pence again was absent for a prolonged stretch when a strained right hamstring sidelined him for 48 games. He ultimately appeared in 106 games, playing enough to re-establish right field as his domain. He made one of the season's most remarkable plays on August 15 against Pittsburgh at AT&T Park when he stumbled on the mound in the visitors' bullpen and caught Josh Harrison's pop-up while falling over backward. Pence, whose oratory in the 2012 postseason served as a rallying cry for the Giants, resumed dispensing his inexhaustible supply of optimism. "See victory where others see nothing," he repeated after the Giants began September by absorbing a galling 5–4 defeat at Chicago.

Center fielder Denard Span proved capable of being an impact player in his first year with San Francisco. He led the Giants in multiple-hit games through much of the season and nicely complemented the outfielders flanking him. Still nagged by the lingering effects of undergoing three surgeries in a nine-month stretch in 2015, Span provided hints of his capabilities when healthy. On May 29, for example, he led the Giants to their 15th victory in 17 games when he drilled three hits, including a home run, and threw out a runner at home plate in an 8–3 victory at Colorado.

Infielder Eduardo Nunez, acquired from the Minnesota Twins shortly before the Trade Deadline, quickly impressed observers with his speed. In fact, many experts believed that Nunez was the Giants' fastest everyday player since Bochy became manager in 2007. As impressive as Nunez looked on the base paths, Bochy particularly appreciated his adaptability. Nunez took over third base after playing primarily shortstop with Minnesota and demonstrated burgeoning expertise at his new spot. "He's making athletic plays, forehand as well as backhand," Bochy said. "And he has a strong arm. I really like the way he's playing third base."

First baseman Brandon Belt needed the "Final Vote" to secure a spot on the NL All-Star team. If only political campaigns were so energetic and thorough. The five candidates in each league all stimulated rousing fan participation from their respective followings. In the end, the tech-savvy Giants organized the socia-media-driven effort to give Belt the push he needed to send him to the Midsummer Classic for the first time. Belt's online vote total reached 10.4 million. A late avalanche of texting and tweeting from his backers enabled him to outpoll Pittsburgh left fielder Starling Marte, Colorado shortstop Trevor Story, Arizona third baseman Jake Lamb, and Milwaukee left fielder Ryan Braun. Bumgarner, Cueto, and Posey were San Francisco's other All-Stars.

ABOUT THE AUTHOR

Chris Haft has covered major league baseball since 1991. He coauthored a book on the Giants' 2010 World Series title, *This Is Our Time*. A native of the San Francisco Bay Area, Haft graduated from Stanford University in 1981 and has two daughters, Samantha and Stephanie.

APPENDIX

World Series Titles
1905
1921
1922
1933
1954
2010
2012
2014

National League Pennants
1888
1889
1904
1905
1911
1912
1913
1917
1921
1922
1923
1924
1933
1936
1937
1951
1954
1962
1989
2002
2010
2012
2014

West Division Titles
1971
1987
1989
1997
2000
2003
2010
2012

Wild-Card Berths
2002
2014
2016

Giants Ballparks
AT&T Park (2000–present)
Candlestick Park (1960–1999)
Seals Stadium (1958–1959)
Hilltop Park (1911)
Polo Grounds III (1891–1957)
Polo Grounds II (1889–1890)
St. George Cricket Grounds (1889)
Oakland Park (1889)
Polo Grounds I (1883–1888)

Retired Numbers
3: Bill Terry
4: Mel Ott
11: Carl Hubbell
20: Monte Irvin
24: Willie Mays
27: Juan Marichal
30: Orlando Cepeda
36: Gaylord Perry
44: Willie McCovey

Baseball Hall of Famers
New York Gothams/Giants

Dave Bancroft
Jake Beckley
Roger Bresnahan
Dan Brouthers
Jesse Burkett
Roger Connor
George Davis
Leo Durocher
Buck Ewing
Frankie Frisch
Burleigh Grimes
Gabby Hartnett
Rogers Hornsby
Waite Hoyt
Carl Hubbell
Monte Irvin
Travis Jackson
Tim Keefe
Willie Keeler
George Kelly
King Kelly
Tony Lazzeri
Freddie Lindstrom
Ernie Lombardi
Rube Marquard
Christy Mathewson
Joe McGinnity
John McGraw
Joe Medwick
Johnny Mize
Hank O'Day
Jim O'Rourke
Mel Ott

Edd Roush
Amos Rusie
Ray Schalk
Red Schoendienst
Bill Terry
John Montgomery Ward
Mickey Welch
Hoyt Wilhelm
Hack Wilson
Ross Youngs

San Francisco Giants

Steve Carlton
Gary Carter
Orlando Cepeda
Rich Gossage
Randy Johnson
Juan Marichal
Willie Mays
Willie McCovey
Joe Morgan
Gaylord Perry
Duke Snider
Warren Spahn

Ford C. Frick Award Recipients
Ernie Harwell
Russ Hodges
Tim McCarver
Lon Simmons
Jon Miller
Lindsey Nelson

Giants Wall of Fame

Felipe Alou
Gary Lavelle
Jim Barr
Johnnie LeMaster
Willie Mays
Rod Beck
Jeffrey Leonard
Vida Blue
Kirt Manwaring
Willie McCovey
Bobby Bolin
Juan Marichal
Jeff Brantley
Jack Clark
Mike McCormick
Bob Brenly
John Burkett
Stu Miller
Bobby Bonds
Orlando Cepeda
Randy Moffitt
Greg Minton
Kevin Mitchell

Will Clark
Mike Krukow
Jim Davenport
John Montefusco
Chili Davis
Matt Williams
Robb Nen
Dick Dietz
Gaylord Perry
Darrell Evans
Jim Ray Hart
Rick Reuschel
J.T. Snow
Tito Fuentes
Kirk Rueter
Scott Garrelts
Robby Thompson
Tom Haller
Chris Speier
Atlee Hammaker
Jeff Kent
Rich Aurilia
Shawn Estes
Marvin Benard